THEODOR SCHWENK

SENSITIVE CHAOS

THE CREATION OF FLOWING FORMS
IN WATER AND AIR

Translated by Olive Whicher and Johanna Wrigley

Illustrations in the text
by Walther Roggenkamp

RUDOLF STEINER PRESS, LONDON, 1965

First English edition, 1965
Second impression, 1971
Third impression, 1976
Fourth impression, 1990

All rights of reproduction and translation
reserved by the original publishers: Verlag
Freies Geistesleben, Stuttgart 1, Haussmannstrasse
76, Germany.

© Rudolf Steiner Press, 1965

ISBN 0 85440 304 3

Printed in England by
Commercial Colour Press,
London E7.

Contents

Ever since that magical moment when my eyes opened under the sea I have been unable to see, think or live as I had done before. That was twenty-six years ago. So many things happened all at once that even now I cannot sort them all out. My body floated weightlessly through space, the water took possession of my skin, the clear outlines of marine creatures had something almost provocative, and economy of movement acquired moral significance. Gravity—I saw it in a flash—was the original sin, committed by the first living beings who left the sea. Redemption would come only when we returned to the ocean as already the sea mammals have done.

When, in the Islands of Cape Verde, Tailliez and I were caught in the nuptial round of the great silver caranx, we were dazzled by the harmonious fluidity of their ballet: as each fish luxuriously adapted the curves of its body in response to the slightest stir of the surrounding water, the whole school regrouped on the pattern of a whirlpool spiral. In the Red Sea, along the coral reefs, I followed with Dumas the big grey sharks, admiring their noble shape but especially the way every part of their body reacted to the impact of the water of which they were the living expression. On the Corsican shelf, 600 feet below, I watched through the portholes of my diving saucer the long seahounds swiftly gliding close to the slime without ever disturbing the clear water.

Off the island of Alboran, above the forests of gigantic laminarians, I dived at night with Falco in the stream of Atlantic waters rushing into the Mediterranean at a speed of three knots. Under the keel of

Espadon we drifted along with our floodlights: all around us there arose from the living sea a hymn to the "sensitive chaos". The vast culture medium was swarming with clusters of eggs, transparent larvae, tiny, faintly coloured crustaceans, long Venus girdles which a single gesture could wind at a distance, crystal bells indolently pulsating, turned by our lights into glittering gems. The salps, small barrel-shaped forms consisting of organised water, were joined together into trains sixty or ninety feet long, their transparency punctuated by the minute orange dots which are at the core of each individual.

All that life around us was really water, modelled according to its own laws, vitalised by each fresh venture, striving to rise into consciousness.

These memories—and many more—have now taken for me a new meaning suggested by the book of Theodor Schwenk. Today it is my privilege to introduce to English readers this remarkable book.

(Translated from the preface of the French edition, 1963)

Foreword

Man's relationship to water has changed completely during the last few centuries. It is now for us a matter of course to have water easily at our disposal for daily use; in the past the fetching and carrying of water involved great effort and labour, and it was valued far more highly. In olden days religious homage was done to water, for men felt it to be filled with divine beings whom they could only approach with the greatest reverence. Divinities of water—the water gods—often appear at the beginning of a mythology.

Men gradually lost the knowledge and experience of the spiritual nature of water, until at last they came to treat it merely as a substance and a means of transmitting energy. At the beginning of the technical age a few people in their inspired consciousness were still able to feel that the elements were filled with spiritual beings. People like Leonardo da Vinci, Goethe, Novalis and Hegel were still able to approach the true nature of water. Leonardo, who may be considered the first man to make systematic experiments with water in the modern sense of the word, still perceived the wonders of this element and its relationship with the developing forms of living creatures. Natural philosophy in the time of Goethe and the Romantic movement still gave water its place as the image of all liquids and the bearer of the living formative processes. People experienced the fluid element to be *the* universal element, not yet solidified but remaining open to outside influences, the unformed, indeterminate element, ready to receive definite form; they knew it as the "sensitive chaos" (Novalis, Fragmente).

The more man learned to know the physical nature of water and to use it technically, the more his knowledge of the soul and spirit of this element faded. This was a basic change of attitude, for man now looked no longer at the *being* of water but merely at its physical value. Man gradually learnt to subject water to the needs of his great technical achievements. Today he is able to subdue its might, to accumulate vast quantities of water artificially behind gigantic dams, and to send it down through enormous pipes as flowing energy into the turbines of the power stations. He knows how to utilise its physical force with astonishing effectiveness. The rising technical and commercial way of thinking, directed only towards utility, took firm hold of all spheres of life, valuing them accordingly.

But what was at first considered with satisfaction to be a great and final achievement is now calling forth a response from nature which asks for second thoughts, and opens up great questions. Whereas it then seemed profitable and advantageous to dry out moors and make them arable, to deforest the land, to straighten rivers, to remove hedges and transform landscapes, today it is being realised that essential, vital functions of the whole organism of nature have very often suffered and been badly damaged by these methods.

A way of thinking that is directed solely to what is profitable cannot perceive the vital coherence of all things in nature. We must today learn from nature how uneconomical and shortsighted our way of thinking has been. Indeed, everywhere a change is now coming about; the recognition of a vital coherence among living things is gaining ground. It is being realised that the living circulations cannot be destroyed without dire consequences and that water is *more* than a mere flow of energy or a useful means of transport.

Humanity has not only lost touch with the spiritual nature of water, but is now in danger of losing its very physical substance. The drying up of countless springs all over the world is a symptom of this development, and the great efforts that are being made on all sides to compensate for the damage done show how serious the situation is. A prerequisite for an effective practical course of action is the rediscovery in a modern form of the forgotten *spiritual nature* of those elements whose nature it is to flow.

This book is intended as a contribution towards this kind of recognition of the nature of the fluid elements. It is concerned mainly with water, the representative of all that is liquid in animate and inanimate nature, and also with the streaming air. As processes of movement in water can, under certain conditions, be imitated in air and vice versa, both water and air may be treated as equivalent in regard to the way they behave when in movement. Therefore in hydrodynamics they are both regarded as "fluids". The qualities they have in common and those that distinguish them from one another will give insight into their real nature.

At first we shall discuss simple phenomena that can be generally observed. These phenomena in water and air may, we think, be regarded as the letters of a script, which it is necessary to learn to use like the alphabet of nature. Those who wish to remain at the stage of pure phenomenology relinquish the ability to read this writing and thus also the ability to understand its meaning. They see the letters, but no words or sentences.

The author wishes to suggest a way on beyond pure phenomenology, towards an ability to "read". The path will be difficult and it will be necessary for the reader to penetrate observantly and patiently into many details until gradually a comprehensive view opens up.

Through watching water and air with unprejudiced eyes, our way of thinking becomes changed and more suited to the understanding of what is alive. This transformation of our way of thinking is, in the opinion of the author, a decisive step that must be taken in the present day.

We would like to add, on a point of method, that we have chosen to use the word "element", rather than "physical condition", because it has a richer content of meaning. It includes the concept of active processes—expressing the essential nature of an element. As we are concerned here not with the chemical compositions but with the *movement* of the flowing elements and the forms which arise through movement, we shall in general not differentiate between water as it appears in nature and the fluids within the living organisms. In particular the movements that are common to them all and which are superior to the differences in substance will be discussed. It will become clear during the course of the book that certain archetypal forms of movement may be found in *all* flowing media, regardless of their chemical composition.

This book is based on scientific observations of water and air but above all on the spiritual science of Rudolf Steiner. In his life's work he has shown how scientific thinking, if carried through logically, can lead to the reality of life and its spiritual origins. And so we would not undertake the attempt to reach an understanding of the spiritual nature of water and air without remembering in gratitude Rudolf Steiner and his tremendous life's work. Further, it would be impossible to write a book like this without an active exchange of ideas with people from all walks of life. I am not forgetful of what I owe to such an exchange of ideas. Many people have supported me with advice and assistance over the years and though it is not possible to mention all their names, it is with gratitude that I remember them here.

I owe special thanks to Helga Brasch for her great help with the writing of the book, and also to Walther Roggenkamp for his considerate cooperation in executing the drawings and the general layout, and to the publishers for their active help in publishing it.

Herrischried in the Black Forest,   *Theodor Schwenk*
Summer 1961

Archetypal Movements of Water

Circulating Systems and Spiralling Surfaces

Wherever water occurs it tends to take on a spherical form. It envelops the whole sphere of the earth, enclosing every object in a thin film. Falling as a drop, water oscillates about the form of a sphere; or as dew fallen on a clear and starry night it transforms an inconspicuous field into a starry heaven of sparkling drops.

We see moving water always seeking a lower level, following the pull of gravity. In the first instance it is earthly laws which cause it to flow, draw it away from its spherical form and make it follow a more or less linear and determined course. Yet water continually strives to return to its spherical form. It finds many ways of maintaining a rhythmical balance between the spherical form natural to it and the pull of earthly gravity. We shall be discussing this play of movement with its rich variety of forms in the following chapters.

A sphere is a totality, a whole, and water will always attempt to form an organic whole by joining what is divided and uniting it in circulation. It is not possible to speak of the beginning or end of a circulatory system; everything is inwardly connected and reciprocally related. Water is essentially the element of circulatory systems. If a living circulation is interrupted, a totality is broken into and the linear chain of cause and effect as an inorganic law is set in motion.

The cycle through the solid, liquid and gaseous phases may be counted among the best known circulatory processes of water. Rising from oceans, lakes and rivers, it circulates with the air in the great atmospheric currents round the earth. Where it enters cooler zones, for instance when rising to pass over a mountain range, it contracts into clouds and falls back to earth as dew, rain, snow or hail. But only a small part—a little more than a third of the precipitation—finds its way towards the sea in streams and rivers. The rest dissolves again into the atmosphere and continues on in the great wandering courses of the low pressure areas or other air currents. In this way water completes a circulation from liquid through vapour

Falling water separates off into drops

back to liquid, which it repeats about thirty-four times during the course of a year. Whether hurrying towards the sea in rivers, whether borne by air currents or falling to the earth as rain or snow —water is always on the way somewhere at some point in one of its great or small circulatory systems. Having seemingly arrived at its goal in the sea, it is swept on by the great ocean currents, in which it continues in its circulation on the surface or in the depths. Currents of gigantic proportions fill the depths of the oceans. The extent of these huge currents is shown by the fact that the oceans account for about 71 per cent of the surface of this earthly planet. When cooled to its point of greatest density, 4°C., water sinks (in salt water conditions are somewhat modified), while warmer water from the depths rises to the surface. On the ocean bed the huge masses of water that have sunk in the polar regions roll towards the equator, and later in far distant places return again to the surface. As we shall see, all stretches of water, every sea and every natural river, have their own circulatory systems.

The plant world plays a special part in the great circulation of water. As plants consist mainly of water a great stream transpires into the atmosphere from fields, meadows and woodlands. On a summer's day a 3,500 gallon stream of water is drawn through an acre of woodland into the atmosphere. In this way the plant world plays a direct part in the great life processes of the earth's organism. It is indeed a most important member of this organism, a channel through which water passes on its great circulating processes over and around the whole earth. For this same reason it is not possible to speak of an independent circulatory system of the plant. The visible streaming of the sap in the plant is only one half of its complete circulation, the other half exists in the atmosphere or in the earth. The plants are vascular systems through which water, the blood of the earth, streams in living interplay with the atmosphere. Together earth, plant world and atmosphere form a *single* great organism, in which water streams like living blood.

What is here spread out over a large space, animal and man have within themselves. What for the plant world is spread in circulation over the face of the whole earth they enclose in a small space, where it moves in just such rhythms and according to just such laws as the water outside in nature.

Just as in man's circulation there are, in the different organs, count-less circulatory systems, which have their own specific tasks to perform, so nature too is full of all manner of great and small circulatory systems, which carry out their own individual tasks and yet are intimately united with the whole. Every healthy lake, every marsh, is a living totality with its own vital functions, while at the same time it belongs to a greater community; it is the organ of a "living being"—the whole surrounding landscape in its own turn is a member of a yet vaster organism.

When we study all this we get a picture of water everywhere vitally active, combining and uniting in creative continuity as it carries out its varied tasks. Not only is it "body", subject to gravity; it is also an *active* element and the foundation of life. We must undertake the rather laborious task of getting to know not only the well known facts about water, but also many of its lesser known qualities.
Looking at a naturally flowing stream we notice the winding course it takes through the valley. It never flows straight ahead. Are these meanderings in the very nature of water?[1] What causes water to follow such a winding course? Its endeavour to complete the circle is here only partially successful, as it cannot flow uphill back to its starting point. Right at the beginning of its circulatory movement it is drawn downhill and in following this downward pull it swings alternately from side to side.

The rhythm of its meanders is a part of the individual nature of a river. In a wide valley a river will swing in far-flung curves, whereas a narrow valley will cause it to wind to and fro in a "faster" rhythm. A brook running through a meadow makes many small often only tentative bends. Stream and surrounding terrain always belong together, and the vegetation unites both in a living totality. In comparison, a river that has been artificially straightened out looks lifeless and dreary. It indicates the inner landscape in the souls of men, who no longer know how to move with the rhythms of living nature.
The meandering flow of water is woven through with a play of finer movements. These result in manifold inner currents which

Naturally flowing water always endeavours to follow a meandering course

[1] The word "meander" comes from a river of this name in Asia Minor, which flows in very pronounced rhythmical loops.

belong intimately to the life and rhythm of a river. As well as the movement downstream there is a revolving movement in the cross-section of the river. Contrary to a first superficial impression the water not only flows downwards but also revolves about the axis of the river.

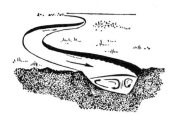

As well as currents flowing downstream there are also revolving currents in the bed of a stream

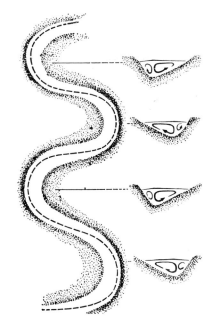

The revolving secondary currents differ in size at the bend of a river. The larger one by the flatter bank on the inside of the curve becomes the smaller one near the steep bank on the outside of the next curve

The direction of this revolving movement results from the fact that the water on the surface flows from the inside of a bend to the outside. There it turns downwards and returns along the bed of the stream to the inner bank, where it rises again to the surface. The two movements together, the revolving circulation and the movement downstream, result in a spiralling motion. A closer examination will in fact usually show that two spiralling streams lie next to one another along the river bed.

Let us look at one point in the current, for instance near the bank on the inside of a bend. On the surface water is streaming outwards; but at the same time spiralling courses rise close by from the bed of the stream to the surface, so that in the stream the different spiralling currents flow through, above and below each other, interweaving from manifold directions. It is like the single strands which, twisted together, make a rope; only here we must imagine that everything is in constant change and also that new water keeps flowing through each single "strand" of water. This picture of strands twisted together in a spiral is only accurate with respect to the actual movement. One does often speak of "strands" of water; they are however not really single strands but whole surfaces, interweaving spatially

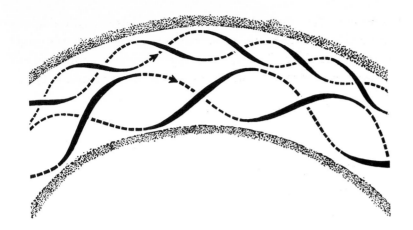

A spiralling movement is caused by the two secondary revolving currents together with the downstream flow (after Möller)

and flowing past each other. The steam over a cup of tea or cigarette smoke as it rises in twisting and turning veils gives a clearer picture of what is meant.

These movements are the cause of the varying degree of erosion of the banks of a water course. The outer banks are always more eroded than the inner, which tend to silt up. The material scooped away from the outer bank wanders with the spiralling current to the inner bank further downstream and is deposited there.

Because of this process the river eats its way further and further outwards at the outer bank, swinging from side to side as it flows, thus making the loops more and more pronounced. They grow closer and closer to the form of a circle, and a flood will complete the process. Then the loops, which have till now contained flowing water, will be by-passed and form so-called backwaters.

Research on canalised rivers, for instance the Rhine in its lower reaches, revealed decades ago that the natural course of water is a

The loops can become so pronounced through erosion that a flood can cause them to be by-passed and left aside as backwaters (after v. Bülow)

rhythmical meandering. Even between straightened banks the river tries, with what remaining strength it has, to realise this form of movement by flowing in a meandering rhythm between the straight banks. Not even the strongest walled banks can hold out indefinitely against this "will" of the water and wherever they offer a chance they will be torn down. The river tries to turn the unnatural, straight course into its own natural one. A meandering motion lengthens the course of the river and thus slows down the speed at which it flows. In this way the river bed is not hollowed out, and the ground-water reserves are left intact.

In straight pipes, too, especially those with an angular cross-section, internal movements come about that are similar to meanders where one would at first assume that the water would flow straight ahead. Separate smaller secondary circulatory systems fill the cross-section of the pipe and together with the main forward flow create moving, spiralling surfaces.

It can happen that parts of the liquid in such a spiralling current on approaching a neighbouring current pass over into it. Here too an interesting movement to and fro in the pipe—after the fashion of a meander—can come about.

Backwaters of the Mississippi
(after Peschel)

Secondary currents also occur in water flowing through straight pipes. They are determined by the shape of the cross-section of the pipe (after Nikuradse)

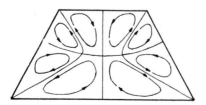

Even where there are no fixed banks to confine the current it flows in rhythmical curves, for instance in the oceans, where whole systems of currents, like the Gulf Stream, flow along in the midst of the ocean waters. The Gulf stream follows its meandering course from the Gulf of Mexico through the Atlantic Ocean to Northern Europe. Warm water flows in the form of a gigantic river in the midst of colder water and builds its own banks out of the cold water itself.[1]

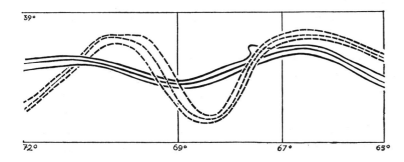

In the Atlantic Ocean the warm Gulf Stream flows through colder water, describing great loops that change their position during the course of time (after Fuglister)

One and the same principle, then, becomes manifest in all dimensions of flowing water, from the small trickle with its little, rhythmical loops, through rivers whose loops grow ever larger, to the loops of the ocean currents surrounding the earth. We see here an archetypal principle of flowing water that wants to realise itself, regardless of the surrounding material. The surrounding material can be on the one hand the hard rock of the mountains, the ice of the glacier with its little channels formed by the water from melting ice, or again, scree, gravel or soil. On the other hand it can consist of warmer or colder water. Regardless of the surrounding material, the current creates for itself a complete, meandering river bed. Even if the surrounding material is organic substance, or even air, the flowing medium still behaves according to the same principle, as we shall show later on. This is a formative principle which appears under the most widely differing physical conditions and is not affected by them. The Gulf Stream is an example not only of this principle of move-

[1] Owing to the easily displaceable nature of such great masses of water the rotation of the earth is of course not without influence. We shall however not go into the complex character of this movement here.

ment in a flowing medium, but also of another ruling principle. The loops of the Gulf Stream shift their position rhythmically to and fro during the course of a long time. Not only are the loops themselves arranged in rhythmical succession but they change their position rhythmically. The Gulf Stream has a rhythmical form in *space,* and it is also subject to a rhythmical process in *time* through the changing position of its loops. The same thing, taking place over lengthy periods of time, can be observed in all natural water courses. This is another expression of the nature of water; it burrows in a rhythmical course into its surroundings in space and is moreover subject to the "course of time" which gradually alters the spatial arrangement of its meanders. The relationship of water to *time* is clearly manifest. We must attempt to reach an understanding of this relationship in order to apprehend the true nature of water, of movement in the organic world and therefore of life itself.

Everywhere liquids move in rhythms. Countless rhythms permeate the processes of nature. Not only are the great currents and tides of the oceans subject to the rhythms of the seasons; every lake, every pond, every well with its ground-water level has its movements that fluctuate with high and low tide or according to other laws.

All naturally flowing waters have their rhythms, perhaps following the course of the day, perhaps keeping time with longer seasonal rhythms. Thus there are times when rivers burrow in the depths, and others when they spread out in width. Lumbermen are well acquainted with this fact. At times the river pushes the logs outward to the banks while at other times they stay in the middle of the waterway.

Let us recapitulate briefly: We demonstrated how water tends to form into spheres; and we saw that even when moving it attempts to retain this spherical principle through circulation. Moving along spiralling surfaces, which glide past one another in manifold winding and curving forms it expresses the conflict between its own natural inclination to the sphere and the force of gravity acting upon it. The current with its rhythmical arrangement in space is subject to greater or lesser rhythms in time, often according to very strict laws. A few examples from the world of living creatures will further illustrate well this inner propensity of water. Every living creature, in the act of bringing forth its visible form out of its archetypal idea, passes through a liquid phase. Some creatures remain in this liquid state or solidify only slightly; others leave the world of water, densify, and fall to a greater or lesser degree under the dominion of the earthly element. All reveal in their forms that at one time they passed through a liquid phase.

The question however arises: Do the forms of the living organisms merely betray the character of the watery phase through which they have passed, or is it that the water itself, impressionable as it is, is subject to living, formative forces and creative ideas of which it is but the visible expression? If so, water as such would be the embodiment of a world of higher forces penetrating through it into the material world and using it to form the living organisms. This is a fundamental question which we shall consider later on; it will in part be answered as we proceed.

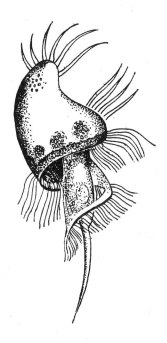

Many unicellular water animals have incorporated the archetypal spiralling movement of water in their shapes. They even usually propel themselves along with a screw-like movement (from Ludwig, after Kahl)

The infusoria are creatures only slightly solidified and hardly differentiated out of their watery surroundings. Many of them reveal the combination of spherical form and direction of propulsion in their screw-like spiralling shapes, which make locomotion possible. The flowing movement of fishes fins is intimately related to the water. Moving as they do like densified veils of water, they embody and make visible the moving forms of the water itself. It is the same principle which comes to expression in organic form, in its function and in the surrounding medium. All three *flow* into one another in movement (Plate 15).

The sketch of the branchial filament of spirographis speaks for itself. A tube-worm native to the Mediterranean, spirographis allows its tentacles to play spirally in the water and when stimulated jerks them spontaneously back into its tube along a screw-like form. Its gill filaments form a perfect spiral.

Spirographis manifests a spirally winding surface even in the delicate build of its gill filaments (after Ludwig)

In the heart of one of the lung-fishes (Protopterus) a dividing wall in the shape of a twisted spiral surface has developed between the two neighbouring blood streams

Secondary currents in the bend of a pipe or of a wide blood vessel

Not only creatures swimming in water but also organs through which water flows are inclined to be spirally formed. In the example of the Gulf Stream we saw that different liquids—for instance warm and cold water—can flow side by side for a long time without any appreciable intermingling. A common example is the confluence of a clear and a muddy stream, where both currents often continue to flow quite a way side by side, separate, yet in close contact along a fairly distinct dividing line.

We see the same phenomenon where arterial and venal blood flow together in the heart and a dividing wall forms where they meet. This dividing wall becomes ever more marked in the advancing sequence of animal development. Though the blood of animal and man is actually a suspension of cells in a liquid, nevertheless phenomena fundamental to a flowing liquid occur here too.

An example is the African lung-fish (Protopterus), in whose heart the dividing wall is an impressive spiralling surface separating the two kinds of blood. As can be seen from the example of the Gulf Stream, the two streams are separate from the start.

The sketch below depicts this process as it occurs in a bent pipe (a wide blood vessel). Following the centrifugal force, the flowing water (blood) pushes towards the outer wall, thus giving rise to two circulations which meet in the central zone. Were a wall to be placed where they meet, the course of the movement would hardly be affected.[1]

We see that a surface remains free into which the living material can grow, making visible what was preformed by movement. The sketch shows this process for the course of the whole bend in the vessel or pipe. The dividing surface which is vertical at entry twists to the horizontal on leaving the bend. If a pipe is painted inside with

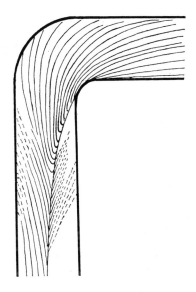

The inside of a bent pipe was painted with a plastic varnish into which the flowing liquid could impress its course (after Hinderks)

a plastic varnish the water flowing through can impress its own course into it. The accompanying sketch shows these courses. If one remembers that the separate courses lie on the cylindrical wall of the pipe, it is clear that they are doubly bent and twisted—like the thread of a screw. Now as the forces of the flowing water simply demand the spiralling form, an elastic vessel will be twisted to a certain extent through the movement of the liquid, and with it also the above mentioned liquid surface of contact. The living material has only to grow into this curled dividing surface in order to make it

---

[1] In *narrow* pipes on the other hand there is always a so-called laminar movement, i.e. water flows in separate layers, parallel in the cross-section, without any appreciable secondary currents or eddies.

In the intestine of Protopterus and other lung-fishes there is also a spiral fold (after Newton Parker)

Spiralling surfaces can be found in the structure of many bones; human humerus

visible. That such spiralling forces actually do occur in elastic vessels with liquid flowing through them can be shown by an experiment with the garden hose-pipe, which writhes back and forth like a snake, when let loose, and cannot be subdued till the end is held steady or the tap turned off. In comparison with the flow of blood these forces are of course much stronger. We shall forbear to analyse this process in greater detail, as we are above all concerned with the forms which arise in flowing liquids. From what we have seen we can already say that such a significant formation as the dividing wall of the heart can be understood out of the movements of the medium flowing through it, and that it is not necessary, as is so often done, to look for utilitarian explanations.

The lung-fishes reveal the already mentioned formative tendency in their intestines. Along the inner wall of the intestine is a well-formed spiral fold, revealing the laws of flowing media in its winding surfaces. The contents of the intestine are of course to a great extent still subject to the laws of liquids.

Let us recall the fact that water endeavours to round itself off into a sphere, to become an image of the whole cosmos. If a directional force is added to this, for instance the force of gravity, then the combination of the two—sphere and directional force—will result in a screw-like or spiralling form.

The child before birth is in a protective envelope of water, prior to his final entry into the sphere of earthly activity. As though lying within a sphere he moulds his as yet liquid form, which gradually becomes more condensed. On being born he leaves the spherical space of water and enters into a relationship with the directional forces of the earth. The more he yields to these forces the more his body becomes solidified, which is essential to standing upright and learning to walk. One of the ways in which his origin in the spherical nature of water—the cosmos—and his orientation towards, and interplay with, the earth are revealed is in the forms of his limbs. The spiralling forms of muscles and bones bear witness to the living world of water and also to a purposeful aim towards mastery of the solid and are reminiscent of the way water flows in meanders and twisting surfaces in the interplay between resting in spheres and being drawn in an earthly direction. (These formative principles are also found in the muscles and bones of the higher animals.)

We have seen how the water in rivers describes curving and twisting surfaces. Such surfaces can be clearly demonstrated by letting water flow out of a container in a wide stream. The stream spirals as the water slips below the edge of the container. This process can often be seen beautifully in fountains where the water falls from basin to basin.

Many limb muscles manifest these spiralling forms. Through the limbs, too, whole systems of currents stream and the muscle more or less follows them. Both muscles and vessels speak of the same thing: streaming movement in spiralling forms. This movement runs through the sinews into the bones. The bone has raised a monument in "stone" to the flowing movement from which it originates; indeed one might say that the liquid has "expressed itself" in the bone.

By a special method, for which we owe acknowledgement to Benninghoff, it is possible to demonstrate the streamlined structure of a bone. Small holes are made with an awl at different points in the decalcified bone and then filled with a coloured liquid, for instance Indian ink. These small holes do not remain round, but in time will be seen to lengthen out, revealing the directions of tension in the bone. If the little fissures are then continued and joined up, the otherwise hidden "systems of currents" in the bone will be made visible. Benninghoff has examined many bones with this method, of which the sketch below is intended to give an impression. These

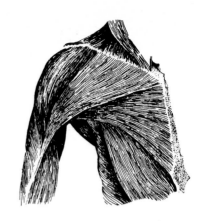

Muscles of the chest and upper arm in the human being

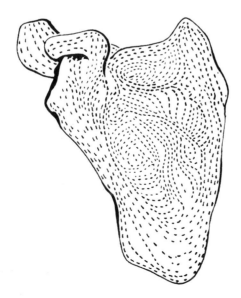

The systems of tiny fissures in many bones show looped and spiralling forms reminiscent of the laws according to which water flows. Human shoulder blade (after Benninghoff)

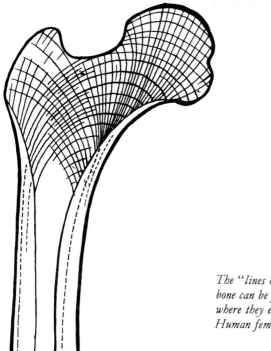

The "lines of flow" on the surface of the bone can be followed right into the interior, where they end in the spongy bone structures. Human femur (after J. Wolff)

systems of currents can be followed right into the bone, where they finally form the familiar spongy bone structures and become incorporated into the static and dynamic forces of standing and walking. Thus again a circle is completed, for statics and dynamics are brought into play by the muscles. And behind them is the invisible human will, which even before any movement becomes visible sends a stream of blood to the muscle which is to be moved. In the quiescent, finished forms of vessels, muscles, ligaments, sinews and bones the same flowing movement can be detected which leads these organs to their varying degrees of density and solidification in such a way that finally in each single organ the underlying spiralling process remains clearly recognisable. And do we not see this flowing movement—in rhythmic sequence—even in the great variety of movements of the human limbs? From what has been said it is however also clear that not all organic forms can be explained simply by the laws of flow. For in the last resort every living form is the expression of an underlying archetypal being.

There is a play of many and diverse kinds of rhythmical movement in rivers, seas and oceans. The most constantly recurring form which meets the eye as it moves, is the wave. It may be observed in every little stream and every river where the water flows over stones or round posts and piers. We have all at one time or another watched the ceaseless onward flow of water: the picture is ever the same, and yet all the time new water is passing by. Here it is parted by a boulder and then unites again, swirling from side to side and creating eddies. There it may be seen jumping over a stone and flowing on in waves. But do the waves flow onwards? Closer inspection will show that the same waves always remain behind the same stone and that the water perpetually flows *through* their constant form. This seems to contradict our usual idea of waves. Mostly they are to be seen wandering over the surface of stationary water; maybe a stone falls into the water and waves spread out in circles, or we watch the ceaseless movement of the incoming tide on the sea shore. Perhaps we sit in a boat and feel the waves passing rhythmically along underneath it, or we may see a piece of wood bobbing up and down on the passing waves without very much altering its position. If however we were to throw a piece of wood into a stream it would be carried away by the current over the waves caused by a stone. This shows that the waves in a flowing stream are totally different from those that wander as a fluctuating movement over still water. The wave behind a stone in a stream remains always at the same place, a lasting form (Plate 2), with new water constantly flowing through it, whereas in the stationary water of a lake or sea the form of the wave is transferred in movement across the surface.

There are, then, two contrasting phenomena:

In a stream: The wave *form* remains at the same spot with new water constantly flowing through it.

In the sea: The wave *form* wanders across the surface, the water itself remaining at the same place.

Through wave movements, of whatever kind, water reveals its extremely impressionable nature. A stone in the stream, a gentle breeze blowing over the surface of a lake, the slightest thing will cause the water to respond immediately with a rhythmical movement. Two things are necessary for this rhythmical movement to come about: the water itself and some other activating force. The actual form of the wave is the result of the interaction of opposing forces, in interplay with one another. The wave is the newly formed third element, arising *between* the polarities—for instance of water and wind—and appears at their surface of contact. Thus water is like a sense organ, which becomes "aware" of the smallest impacts and immediately brings the contrasting forces to a moving rhythmical balance.

With both kinds of waves, those through which the water flows and those which themselves travel over the surface, it is possible for different systems of waves to be superimposed upon one another. Plate 3 shows that on the main waves caused by stones which happen to be lying at the edge of the stream there are smaller waves caused by the surface tension of the water.

Wave trains coming from different directions interpenetrate each other, causing interference patterns. Strictly regular patterns and structures may come about in both types of wave. Plate 6 shows examples of surface tension waves in front of thin sticks in a natural stream. In this case the waves remain at the same place and new water constantly flows through them. It is interesting to note the structures which occur where the wave systems meet and cross each other.

Interference patterns also occur with travelling waves. In the large expanses of the open sea and given sufficient wind force they can cause huge pyramid-shaped mountains of water to form where they intersect. These interference patterns can often be observed at headlands, where waves from different directions meet, and their agitation and very concentrated force is sometimes a danger to shipping.

The above-mentioned phenomenon—different wave systems superimposed upon one another—plays an important part in nature. It shows that the most varied *movements* can occur at one and the same place in *space*. In the case of solid bodies there can be no question of intersection or interpenetration. Where there is one solid body there can be no other. It is however possible for there to be a diversity of movements and rhythms all in one place. There can be in one place only *one* solid body but *many* and diverse movements. This is an important universal principle; structures are imposed upon space, arranging and dividing it up according to systematic laws. This shows movement to be independent of space, though *appearing* in it as a regulating principle.

Every movement has a certain speed, its own characteristic speed. A movement is given character by being either fast or slow, sluggish or active, brisk or hesitant. Still more characteristic of a movement is its rhythm; we can learn much about the beings of nature through the rhythms which are an integral part of them.

In the realm of water the same applies. The individual nature of any stretch of water is given an unmistakable character by the speed, size and rhythm of its wave formations. An experienced seaman can tell by the character of the waves rolling up, where they are from and what caused them. It can happen for instance that waves of an ocean swell originating in a storm at the southernmost point of America roll towards the south-west coast of England. They are waves which have detached themselves from a local gale zone—in

Longer waves overtake the shorter ones and hasten on ahead (after H. Walden)

this case South America—and after a long journey eventually reach the coasts of Europe. Great waves like this occur when a strong wind blows for a long time across large stretches of water. Waves of great length can arise (the length of a wave is the distance between the crests of two successive waves). When a wind rises, the surface of the sea will at first become ruffled and then gradually bigger and bigger waves will form. The first ones with short wavelengths will have travelled a long way before those with long wavelengths have formed. But even so the large waves will catch up with and overtake the small ones because the long waves which have formed later have a greater speed of propagation. As they move along an interesting sorting out takes place. The long waves, which have been formed last, hurry forward at their greater speed, the shorter ones follow and the shortest, which are the oldest, come last of all. But the shortest will long have outrun their energy while the long ones still hurry on across great distances.

The individual nature of a stretch of water is expressed in the waves which arise in it and vibrate in various harmonies and rhythms. To the peculiar nature of a stretch of water belongs also an individual movement which fluctuates with a slower, more extended rhythm, while bearing on its surface the more delicate play of waves caused by the wind. Every water basin, whether ocean, lake or pond, has its own natural period of vibration. This varies according to the shape, size and depth of the basin. The whole morphological character of a lake finds expression in this natural period of vibration; it is like a "note" to which the lake is "tuned". This "note" has "overtones" in its vibration, like a flute or the string of a musical instrument. Like these the lake oscillates between the nodes (regions of no disturbance) and the anti-nodes (regions of maximum disturbance) of standing waves. The "overtones" are not to be confused with the above-mentioned equally characteristic play of smaller waves on the surface. The natural period of vibration of a stretch of water is in more or less marked resonance with the path of the moon and its tide producing forces. The resonance is strongest when the natural period of vibration corresponds to the orbital rhythm of the moon. It is then as with a child's swing, which if pushed according to its natural rhythm—for instance always at its highest point—requires only a small effort to keep it swinging. In the same way a lake already in fluctuation—for instance through sudden local changes in the atmospheric pressure—will be the more easily moved the nearer its natural period of vibration is to the rhythm of the moon's path. As the moon wanders over the different waters of the earth, they respond to a greater or lesser degree with their "note" according to how closely their natural period of vibration is tuned to the rhythm of the moon. All together they are like a great musical instrument, spread out over the earth, on which the moon plays an inaudible melody, which wanders with it round the earth.

To the two kinds of wave movement already mentioned we may, then, add a third: the standing wave of the natural period of vibration of a stretch of water. The standing wave—like the travelling waves which spread rhythmically over the surface—does not involve a forward-moving current. A current may of course be produced when standing waves encounter a flat beach. On a large scale the tides involve currents of this kind. Hindrances will also give rise to waves through which the water is actually flowing, as in the waves of a brook. We see this type of rhythmic flow on every flat beach, where the sand is shifted to and fro by the oncoming waves and, in the wake of rocks or stones, wave forms with water flowing through them can arise.

On the beach rhythmical wave movements turn into a rhythmical *ebb and flow*. Flowing movements can also be superimposed upon a rhythmically progressing wave; for instance a wave bears forward moving currents on its back when the wind blows so strongly that the water on the surface itself begins to move. Then the water flowing on the top of the wave moves faster than the wave itself, overshoots the crest and falls into the trough beyond. In this way one layer of water can slide over another. This causes the layers to curl over and turn in upon themselves, creating foaming breakers. The same happens when high waves hurry towards the shore; the speed of the lower layers of water is impeded, so that the faster upper layers over-shoot the crest and break.

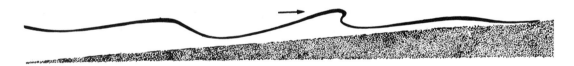

A wave flowing up the beach

The movements which occur within the water as a rhythmically progressing wave passes can be made visible by a suspension of small particles in the water. Each of these will be seen to make small circling movements as the crest and trough of the wave pass. Every particle remains more or less where it is, but describes a small circle.

A wave does not generally create a forward moving current. As the wave passes, the water simply moves in circles

Every wave therefore causes an inconceivable number of small circular movements, which touch, intersect and interpenetrate. When the waves enter shallow water these small circles stretch out and turn into ellipses, which become more and more elongated as the water grows shallower. With these ellipses in shallow water the

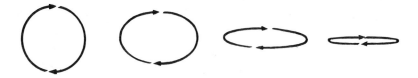

When a wave flows up a flat beach the circular movements become first elliptical and then finally ebbing and flowing currents

original circular movement of the deep water becomes more and more the ebb and flow that can be observed on a flat beach.

Flow phenomena caused by rhythmical processes can be created experimentally, if for instance a vessel of water is subjected to oscillating, to and fro movements. More or less complicated, though regular currents are brought about, the form of which depends on the kind of rhythm used (frequency, intensity, amplitude, etc.).

This whole realm of moving forms and formative movements bears

In oscillating containers filled with water, geometrically regular patterns of flow occur, varying according to the shape of the container (after Parlenko)

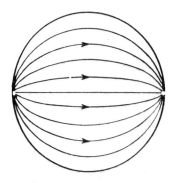
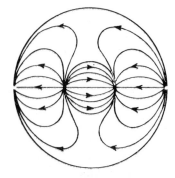

closely upon the creative principles and living processes at work in the organic kingdoms of nature.

For instance, when a wave appears and remains stationary behind a stone in a stream, a form is all the time being created simply out of movement, with new substance constantly flowing through it. This is an archetypal principle of all living creation—an organic form, in spite of continuous chemical change, remains intact.

Again, in rhythmically progressing waves the form moves over the liquid, which remains in one place. This liquid is thereby thoroughly "kneaded" by an inconceivable interplay of small movements and extensive inner surfaces are formed. The wave is the newly created third factor in the interplay between two forces, always revealing a moving balance between them. It is always latent in the still, balanced surface of water, appearing at the slightest stimulation. Its dimensions correspond to the dimensions of the forces at work and so does its speed of propagation: long waves travel faster than short waves, and in the process the waves are sorted out according to wavelengths. We shall meet a corresponding principle in the realm of sound in connection with the process of hearing. The speed of a rhythm, like the speed of movements, expresses something of the inner nature of a living being.

Yet again, when different wavelengths intermingle with one another, patterns, structures and formations arise, which originate purely out of movement. At every single point, where wave trains from different directions meet, spatial forms arise such, for instance, as pyramid-shaped structures or interweaving organic-looking surfaces

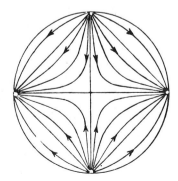  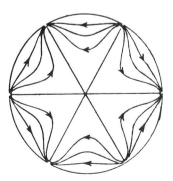

and the like. It is possible for water to create forms out of the interplay of various forces or directions of movement. This is a principle which plays a great part for instance in all embryonic processes. In all things great and small the whole of nature is inter-woven with interpenetrating rhythms and movements, and forms are created in the interplay between them. Form patterns such as those appearing in waves with new water constantly flowing through them, picture on the one hand the creation of form and on the other the constant change of substance in the organic world.

Thus we see that right from the first, the fluid element contains moving, formative processes akin to those which living beings use to form their bodies. The creation of form in living substance is only thinkable if at one and the same place in space manifold movements can flow into, over and through one another. The fluid element is thus a most suitable medium for the form-creating process, which would be impossible in the three dimensional world of solids, where there is only exclusiveness and no interpenetration. Nature here reveals one of her secrets, showing how movements are indeed by their very nature "super-spatial"; they do not exclude one another at one and the same point in space but interpenetrate and move over and under one another. They appear in the spatial world as though from higher realms and in so doing create law and order. The fluid element is therefore the ideal bearer of movements, by which it allows itself to be moulded and plasticised.

Rhythmical waves and flowing currents are two different elements of movement in water, but they can change over into one another or be superimposed one upon the other and work together. Fluid flow can arise through rhythms, and—as we shall see later—rhythms can also arise through flow movements. Here again is an important principle which nature applies in the creation of her living creatures out of the fluid medium. It has for instance been observed that in the hen's egg the inner formative processes in the embryo are accompanied by rhythmical wave movements. These run in a gentle wave of contractions over the amnion of the egg from one end to the other and back. It is a kind of rhythmical to and fro movement which continuously massages and moulds the content of the egg. Let us recall how as a wave moves along, the substance carrying it, though remaining in the same place, is permeated by countless small movements which interpenetrate with one another in the most varied ways. Experiments have shown that this principle can be used artificially; even in unfertilised eggs, the development of the embryo may be initiated by rhythmical shaking.[1]

The interrelationship of the forward flowing movement and rhythm is seen in the blood circulation of the higher animals and of man. How characteristic of the living being is either the heavy, sluggish circulation of the elephant or the quick vibrating rhythm of a small animal, say the humming-bird!

Rhythmical wave movements are transformed into straight currents by the cilia of the lower water creatures. Through the wave-like rhythm of the cilia the animal either creates a current around itself or propels itself along in the water. In the ciliated epithelia of several organs of the higher animals and man similar processes take place, only they do not serve the purpose of propulsion but are intended to transport substances within the body. Fishes create currents through rhythmical wave-like movements and thus propel themselves along. This is most evident in fish which have continuous fins, for instance the electric eel or the common sole, which have one continuous fin from head to tail (Plate 15). A similar example is the ray, which has a "built in" wave movement in its wing-like lateral fins. Waves move from front to back over the surface of its fins. It pushes the wave enclosed by its fin backwards and as a result swims forward. Many water creatures have incorporated the archetypal movements of water into the shape of their bodies, some more than others. The ray shows this to perfection.

In animals such as the snakes, the archetypal wave movement comes to expression in the movement of the whole body. This shows beautifully when they swim; the waves in the water merge with the wave-like movement of the animal to form a single unity (Plate 14). How great a part is played by the wave-rhythm in many living creatures is shown by the peristaltic processes in the intestines. They are wave-like, to-and-fro movements which take place unceasingly in the intestines; their cessation would endanger the life of the organism to which they belong.

The ray has assimilated the movement of the waves into its fin movements (after Hesse-Doflein)

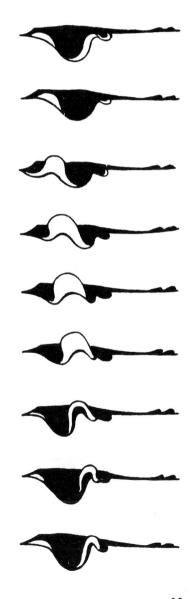

[1] This can however also be done by chemical stimuli; these are much closer to rhythmical movement than may at first be supposed. We shall return to this later.

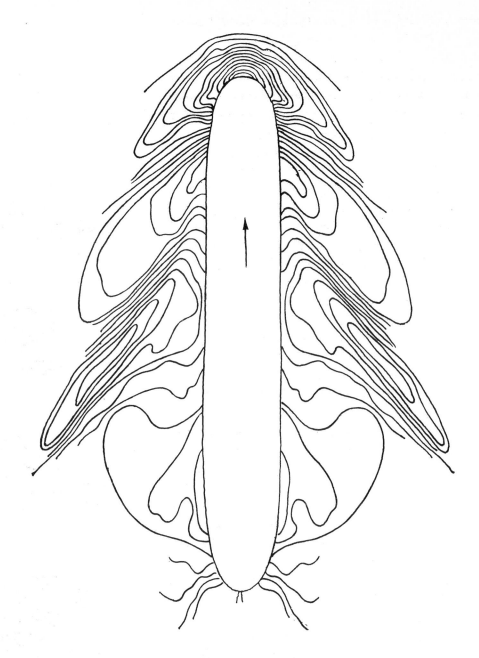

*A fish-shaped object drawn through water
causes waves that can be particularly clearly
depicted in contour-lines (after Handbook
of Experimental Physics)*

All that is rhythmical in the nature of a wave, where the contiguous elements—water and air for example—remain separate, becomes altered as soon as the wave begins to break. It folds over and curls under, forming hollow spaces in which air is imprisoned in the water. The elements, which have till now been separate, unite in turbulence and foam, overlapping and forming hollow spaces. At the same time the foaming water disintegrates into vapour, entering the air in a rhythmical succession of misty clouds.

Wherever hollow spaces are formed, when upper layers of water overshoot the more slowly moving lower layers, the water is drawn into the hollows in a circular motion. Eddies and vortices arise. If we could watch the process in slow motion we would see how a wave first rises above the general level of the water, how then the crest rushes on ahead of the surge, folds over and begins to curl under. This presents us with a new formative principle: the wave folding over and finally curling under to form a circling vortex.

Dividing surfaces or boundary layers appear not only between water and air, but also in the midst of water itself, for instance at the confluence of two rivers, or where the water is parted by an obstacle and then meets again. Here too a surface of contact arises where the two meet. Where streams of water flow past each other at different speeds we also find surfaces of contact; like the surface between water and air, these surfaces will become waved, overlap and finally curl round (Plate 23). We are here concerned with the processes taking place at the actual surface of contact, and not with their position in space, which may be horizontal or vertical. The processes at these boundary surfaces are in every case the same as those on the surface of water: the wave-formation, the overlapping and the curling round of the layers. These processes can be more easily observed when the boundary surfaces are vertical; when they are horizontal, as in the natural wave formation described above, the process of vortex formation takes place much more under the influence of gravity and therefore the whole thing is more liable to collapse in foam.

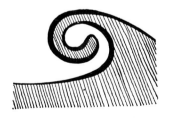

A wave curls over to form a vortex

In every naturally flowing stream we can see what happens at the boundary surfaces, where for instance a twig from a bush on the bank hangs into the water, or where the water has to flow round a stone. The flowing water is parted by the obstruction and unites again when it has passed. But the little obstruction causes a cleavage, a dividing line, a boundary surface in the water, which bulges out into a wave alternately to one side and then the other, folds over and curls into a vortex. On both sides of the boundary surface a series of small alternate vortices arises, which travel downstream with the current.

In a clear stream the vortices appear as small round hollows, in which sometimes small bits of wood or pollen spin round. If the sun shines on the water they are projected as small circular discs in a regular pattern on the bed of the stream.

A distinct train of vortices (after Homann)

Wherever currents of water meet, after a single current has been parted by an obstacle, for instance by bridge piers, or when two different streams meet, the confluence is always the place where rhythmical and spiralling movements may arise (Plate 23). Also where water flows into a lake the same rhythmical movements and vortices occur at the boundary surface between the moving water of the stream and the still water of the lake. Every curving movement in the boundary surface may lead to the formation of an entirely new form, which lives its own individual, whirling life within the current of water, namely, the circling vortex (Plate 37).

Boundary surfaces of the kind we have been describing occur wherever there are flowing currents, but they are usually invisible, for they do not show up in clear transparent water.

It can be observed that in every stream the water at the edges flows more slowly than in the middle. In other words, faster layers flow past slower layers and this means that very extensive inner surfaces come about as layer after layer flows by. The same can be observed in pipes. In the thinnest pipes, where there can be no question of vortices, the layers at the edge move considerably more slowly than those in the centre (laminar flow). (Some idea of the development of inner surfaces, as these layers flow past each other, can be gained if one imagines how the pages of an unbound book slide over each other when they are bent back and forth.) If the difference in speed between neighbouring layers reaches a certain degree, vortex formations occur. These always originate in the surfaces of contact between different elements concerned in the movement, for example something resting and something moving, a hard edge and the flowing water, and so on. So-called turbulence in a current of water has to do with the instability of these surfaces of differentiation in relation to the speed of the flow.

This is the archetypal phenomenon of vortex formation. Wherever any qualitative differences in a flowing medium come together, these isolated formations occur. Such differences may be: slow and fast; solid and liquid; liquid and gaseous. We could extend the list: warm and cold; denser and more tenuous; heavy and light (for instance,

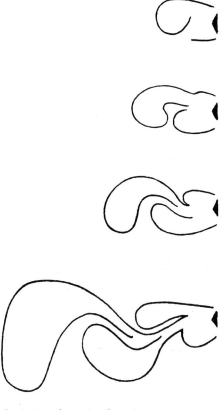

Beginning of a train of vortices (after Walter)

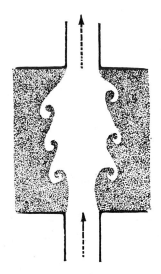

Whirling, mingling movements occur when warm water streams into cold or vice versa

salt water and fresh); viscous and fluid; alkaline and acid. . . . At the surfaces of contact there is always a tendency for one layer to roll in upon the other. In short, wherever the finest differentiations are present the water acts as a delicate "sense organ" which as it were perceives the differentiations and then in a rhythmical process causes them to even out and to merge.

39

The formation of vortices occurs on a large scale where great masses of water of different temperatures meet. Mingling currents off Newfoundland

The full development of a wave leads to the overlapping and rolling in of layers of water, resulting in circling moving forms which lie isolated in the general current and travel with it. In the undulating, to and fro movement, which persists as long as the wave retains its form, neighbouring media of differing qualities only touch; but they intermingle thoroughly as soon as the wave form breaks and creates hollow spaces in which for instance air is enclosed, as in breakers on a beach or vortices in a current. Not only air, other substances may of course become imprisoned in the hollow spaces, depending on what opposing elements are in contact *before* the inward curling movement occurs. As soon as different media, even different qualities within the *same* medium, flow together, for instance warm and cold water, the one is taken into the other so that the hollow space, like a vessel, is filled with water of a different quality. The important thing here is that *hollow forms* arise, which can be filled with another medium, just like any receptacle.

The hollowing out of inner spaces is a fundamental process—an archetypal form-gesture in all organic creation, human and animal, where in the wrinkling, folding, invaginating processes of gastrulation, organs for the development of consciousness are prepared. Forms arising out of this archetypal creative movement can be found everywhere in nature.

Early stage in the development of the human embryo (after Clara)

This important phenomenon—the curling in of folds or layers to create a separate organ with a *life of its own* within the whole organism of the water—does actually occur in the forming of organic structures. The differences of speed in the fluid flow correspond to the different speeds of growth or development in an organic form. Slower or more rapid growth of neighbouring layers leads to the overlapping, folding, involuting and invaginating in the process of which the organs are developed. Like vortices, organs have their own life: they are distinct forms within the organism as a whole and yet in constant flowing interplay with it. A great example of this process is the pupa of a butterfly. The organs, at first curled up, are pushed out when fully developed and appear as feelers, limbs or the like.

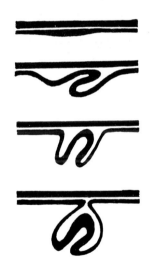

In the rigid chrysalis of a butterfly, growth takes place at varying speeds. This leads to folding processes in preparation for the forming of the organs (from Eidmann, after Weber)

The first stages of this archetypal movement also occurs in the plant world. At the growing tip wave-like bulges appear which later fold over and develop into leaves which open up into the air. In general the plant stops short of the actual vortex development. Only in the forming of the blossoms is there a suggestion of inner hollow spaces; there we are reminded of the world of butterflies and insects—in

Shoot of an alga (after Goebel)

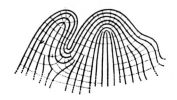

fact, of animal development. Indeed, we often see the plant even unfurling from the spiralling form into the flat, expanding form of the leaf, for example, in the fern (Plate 44).

Boundary surfaces, with their rhythmical processes, are birthplaces of living things. It is as though the creative, formative impulses *needed* the boundary surfaces in order to be able to act in the material world. Boundary surfaces are everywhere the places where living, formative processes can find a hold; be it in cell membranes, surfaces of contact *between* cells, where the life forces are mysteriously present; in the great boundary surfaces between the current systems of the oceans, where various currents flow past each other in different directions—these are known to be particularly rich in fish; or in the infinitely extensive surfaces of the natural and artificial filter systems of the earth, where the water seeping through is purified and given back its vital qualities.

Leaf nodes at the growing tip
(after Sachs)

A similar process akin to the formation of organs must have taken place in the great stages of development of the planet earth, when it was still in a fluid state, processes which are today so to speak petrified and at rest in the crust of the earth. They are to be found in many places in the mountain ranges, or inside the earth—for instance in excavations. They point to youthful stages in the development of the earth, when it was obviously still permeated by

Folding on the surface of the earth: the great mountain ranges of Central Europe and North Africa

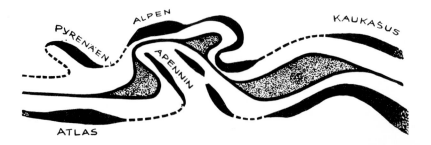

living organic processes. In his book *Lebensstufen der Erde*, W. Cloos describes these early life processes of the planet earth in a grand panoramic review of geology. These formative principles can be traced right into the fine structure of the rock, in which the great processes—creating and assorting matter—have as it were projected themselves. We can come to understand them by learning to know the archetypal movements of all living matter and the movements of water—the element of life. The whole globe must have been penetrated through and through with these life-processes in the distant past.

Vertical section of the Alps in the region of the Simplon Pass. Length of the section about 16 miles, depth about 6 miles (after C. Schmidt)

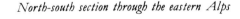

North-south section through the eastern Alps

Vortex funnel

All flowing water, though it may seem to be entirely uniform, is really divided into extensive inner surfaces. If vortices form behind a stone or a bridge pier, these layered inner surfaces will of course also be drawn into the whirlpool, flowing past each other in a circular or spiral course. As water is transparent this process is difficult to observe unless colouring matter is used. Then one can see how the inside of the vortex turns faster than the outer part, and how the revolving layers glide past each other (Plate 37). It is a form which has separated itself off from the general flow of the water; a self-contained region in the mass of the water, enclosed within itself and yet bound up with the whole.

Closer observation reveals that this vortex has a rhythm of its own. Contracting at one moment, it stretches itself downward, extending with its lower end right into the depths; at the next, expanding in breadth, it draws up the tapering inner layers again. Then follows a renewed contraction, together with an extension downward, which is again withdrawn to spread out in breadth and so on. It is a rhythmic pulsation.

A picture of the process can be gained by causing water in a cylindrical vessel to whirl round so that a funnel-shaped vortex arises, to which a drop of colour is added. It is then easy to see how the outside layers turn more slowly than those inside and how the whole form pulsates rhythmically up and down. Especially the inner layers describe corkscrew-like surfaces which become more pronounced as the movement slows down. This archetypal movement of water in spirally winding surfaces has already been described in the first chapter.

We come to realise that the vortex is a figure complete in itself with its own forms, rhythms and movements. On closer examination we find that the vortex with its different speeds—slow outside, fast inside—is closely akin to the great movements of the planetary system. Apart from minor details, it follows Kepler's Second Law of planetary movement: a given planet circles round the sun as though in a vortex in as much as it moves fast when near the sun and slowly when further away. This law applies to the whole planetary system, from the planets nearest the sun to those furthest away. The vortex in its law of movement is thus a miniature image of the great planetary system. Its outer layers, like the planets

Water around a whirlpool moves in spirals

furthest from the sun, move more slowly than its inner layers, which circle more quickly round the centre, like the planets nearer to the sun. The sun itself would correspond to the centre of the vortex. Strictly speaking the "circling" of the planets is of course eccentric.

The vortex has yet another quality that suggests cosmic connections. If a very small floating object with a fixed pointer is allowed to circle in a vortex, the pointer always points in the direction in which it was originally placed, that is, it always remains parallel to itself! In other words it is always directed to the same point at infinity. It can of course be started off pointing in any direction and it will then remain pointing in this direction while circling in the vortex. This shows how a vortex is orientated—as though by invisible threads— with respect to the entire firmament of fixed stars.

A small piece of wood circling in a vortex. It constantly points in the same direction

The vortex is, therefore, a system depicting in miniature the great starry universe; its orientation in space corresponds to the fixed stars and its inner laws of movement to the solar system with its planets. The sun itself corresponds to the suction centre of the vortex, where the speed is theoretically infinitely great. But as infinitely great speeds are not possible on earth, the dense water vaporises in the suction centre, which is then filled with air, the substance next in density. This is sucked into the screw-like spirals of the vortex in a pulsating rhythm (Plate 41).

In his book *Technische Strömungslehre* Eck characterises the processes in the suction centre of a vortex: "If $r = 0$ then $p = -\infty$ (in words: if the radius is 0, i.e. at the absolute centre of the vortex, then the pressure is minus infinitely great. The author). We are thus forced to acknowledge a negative pressure, that is a pressure less than in a vacuum (not to be confused with 'low pressure'). What does this mean? The pressure we have dealt with up to now was tension, i.e. a force directed to the centre of a body, and working positively. It will be easiest to imagine a negative pressure if we think of the theory of solids. Negative pressure is here none other than suctional tension. The same applies to liquids. But in general the liquid would disintegrate and vaporise before reaching this point."

A description by Rudolf Steiner, arising out of his spiritual scientific research, of the conditions at the centre of the sun is interesting in this connection:

"Imagine we have some kind of filled space—we will call it A and place a plus sign in front of it (+A). Now we can make the space emptier and emptier, whereby A gets smaller and smaller; but there is still something in the space, therefore we still use the + sign. We can imagine that it could be possible to create a space which is entirely empty of air, although this is not possible under earthly conditions because a space can only be made approximately empty. Were it possible, however, to make a space entirely void, it would contain nothing but space. Let us call it nought; the space has zero contents. Now we can do with the space as you can do with your purse. When you have filled your purse you can take out more and more, until at last there is nothing left in it. If then you still want to go on spending money, you cannot take out any more, but you can make debts. But if you have made debts there is less than nothing in your purse:

$$+A \qquad O \qquad -A$$

This then is how you can imagine the space—not only empty, but one might say sucked out, filled with less than nothing ($-A$). It is this kind of sucked out space—a space which is not only empty, but just the opposite of being filled with substance—that one must imagine the space to be which is taken up by the sun. Within the sun there is suction—not pressure, as in a gas-filled space, but suction. The sun is filled with negative materiality. I give this as an example to show that earthly laws cannot so simply be applied to cosmic regions. . . ." (From a lecture given on 24th June, 1921.)

In general we know water only according to its earthly laws. The build up of a vortex shows us that water is also governed by cosmic laws. We shall later go into this less familiar aspect of water in more detail.

The vortex is a moving part within a moving whole; it has its own rhythms, forms its own inner surfaces and is connected with distant cosmic surroundings. These qualities relate it to the realm of organic creation. It is a separate entity within a streaming whole, just as an organ in an organism is an individual entity, yet closely integrated with the whole through the flow of vital fluids. An organ is orientated in relation to the whole organism and also to the surrounding cosmos; yet it has its own rhythms and forms inner surfaces of its own.

All the different stages of the formation of a vortex, from the commencement of overlapping to the completed curling in of the layers of water, serve Nature in her formative creativity. During the course of development every organism and each of its organs must pass through a liquid state. The various possibilities of movement offered by the vortex present a direction along which an organ may develop before it eventually acquires its own individual nature and

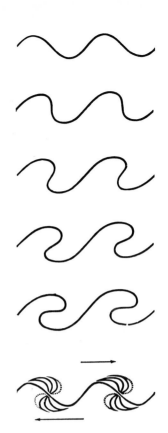

The surface of contact between two currents curls over to form a vortex
(after Bjerknes)

specialised function. The vortex in the water is completely unspecialised, and remains as pure movement at a primitive, undifferentiated stage of development. It is like an archetypal organ—an Ur-organ —having within it all potentialities of differentiation and formation. We can here see how the formative processes used by Nature for her various creations are pictured in the first place in the element of water as movements.

Some examples will elucidate this. First let us consider an example in which the vortex hardly appears as a form but is functionally present, guiding the formative process. In the embryo development

Development of the hypophysis in the sand lizard. The surrounding material curls in around the hypophysis as centre. Compare previous sketch (after Gawrilenko, simplified)

47

of a species of lizard the formation of the hypophysis, an endocrine gland, commences at a certain point. Through certain growth processes in the head region of the embryo a kind of curling under takes place.

The above sketch shows the head end of the embryo and the position of the hypophysis. The two stages of the process are sufficient to show how the hollow at the place in question deepens and the curling in of the head region becomes more pronounced. If these separate stages are observed together we see how the whole head region is curved round the hypophysis as centre. The hypophysis here corresponds to the centre of the vortex itself, the surrounding material is "whirled in" around it. In this example the vortex form is not itself an organ, but as a process it dominates the whole development of the future organ.

If we take into consideration that the hypophysis is the organ which controls all growth, we may correctly presume that in the formative processes here described it is active as an invisible centre from which the growth processes *of all other organs* are guided. Taking also into account the connection between vortex movements and cosmic space, we find here the picture of a superior type of centre which creates other organs—a microcosmic world—around itself.

Instead of a complete system of semicircular canals the river-lamprey has one semicircular canal and two spiral cavities in which the liquid is kept circulating by cilia (after De Burlet)

In the following example, a vortex movement in a liquid serves as an "organ" without solidifying into a solid form. In the river-lamprey we find a preliminary stage of the development of the semicircular canals in higher animals. Here, two out of the three semicircular canals are circling vortices in a liquid, each in its own cavity. They are set in motion by ciliated epithelia. If the interior of the cavities were to be filled with a dense substance, the membranous or bony semicircular canal would arise, as in the higher animals. In the river-lamprey the centre of the vortex is not yet filled in and the circulating liquid in the cavities is free to move. Like the semicircular canals, it serves as a sense organ and gives the animal a sensation of its position in space. What in the higher animals has solidified out into an organic form, is here still recognisable as a freely moving liquid in a vortex. The organ of the higher animal may be regarded as solidified movement; within it the movements of the liquid take place which lead to sense impressions.

The example which shows the vortex as an organic form at rest is the human cochlea, situated close to the semicircular canals. It is as though its dynamic force had entered into this most finely developed form. We shall return later to these processes in the inner ear itself. These three examples show different stages at which the vortex may reveal itself, ranging from an invisible creative dynamic principle to an organ in all its finest detail. All the intervening stages and manifold variations of the vortex formation can be discovered everywhere in nature.

The multitude of snails and shells, some spiral formations in the plant world and even the structure of many crystals speak of the vortex form and its dynamic force (Plates 42 and 43).

The form of the vortex, with its quality of creating a connection with the surrounding world, appears in the horns of many animals. Horns may often be regarded as delicate sense organs, which guide

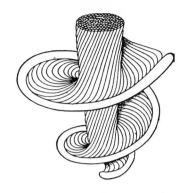

Fibres in the auditory nerve, arranged spirally just like a liquid vortex, as though picturing an invisible vortex of forces (after De Burlet)

Cochlea and semicircular canals in the human being (after Rauber-Kopsch)

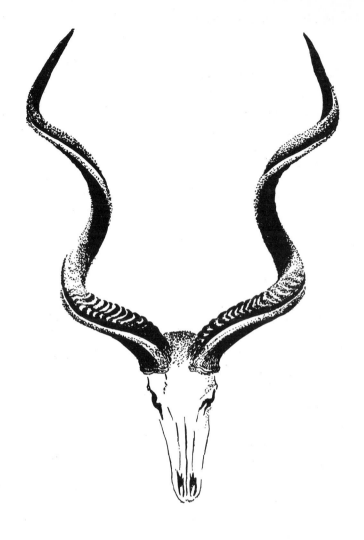

Horns of the African kudu antelope

the animal. The sketch shows the horns of the kudu, an African antelope. The twisting is clearly visible and also the axis round which the "vortex" spirals.

Here too the form of the vortex seems to hover invisibly over the growth processes, even before the horns are actually there, for they proceed along this spiral path with mathematical exactitude in their annual growth. It is significant that the axes of the two spiralling horns meet either in the nose or by the eyes or in their immediate vicinity, a fact which stresses the strong connection of the horns with sense perception and with the animal's sense of its surroundings. Furthermore, in structure the horn, like the water vortex, is finely laminated, layer upon layer.

A blade of grass or a twig dangling in the water causes a series of small vortices to form, which travel on downstream with the current. They are hardly visible, unless the sun shines through the clear water on to the bed of the stream, when they are projected, as already described, as small discs of shadow which move on in a regular pattern. On the surface of the water the vortices look like small hollows, in which a splinter of wood, or maybe a small leaf or some pollen, spins round. With the help of suitable additions to the water it is possible, just as with a single vortex, to make a train of vortices visible. Then the rhythmical pattern of the whole formation can be clearly seen (Plate 23).

United by a meander winding its way between them, the vortices alternate in corresponding pairs, one slightly ahead spinning one way and the other, behind, spinning the other way. If the stream flows slowly, only the meandering surface of contact arises. But the rhythmical train of vortices, formed out of the wavy rhythm and curling movement of the dividing surface, becomes more and more pronounced the faster the stream flows. This also explains the alternation which usually occurs in the pairs of vortices in a vortex train. In the moment of formation the two vortices lie opposite each other; only when the whole train has swirled into its final "stable" position do they lie alternately, one behind and still slightly to the side of its pair.

A similar process takes place if a small rod, held vertically, is drawn through still water. This method can be used for the study of trains of vortices, of which Plates 25–28 are examples. Plate 29 shows the preliminary wave formation caused by slow movement of the rod, and Plate 28 the completed curling process. Plates 25 and 27 demonstrate the differences in the vortex train caused by rods of different shapes and sizes. The rhythm in which the vortices follow one another varies according to the width of the rod: narrow rods cause short intervals between the vortices, wide rods cause longer intervals and therefore fewer vortices for a stretch of the same length, provided that the speed of the current or the movement of the rod is the same in all cases.

In order to make the vortex trains visible with such clarity, a viscous fluid was mixed with the water, slowing down the course of the movement and thus making the process easily discernible even

Rhythmical arrangement of vortices in water

to the naked eye. It is clear from Plates 25–28 that a train of vortices is a totality whose separate members are held together by strict rhythmical laws.

If one examines the whole field of motion of a train of vortices, for instance as in Plate 26, one notices that the single vortices are clearly separated from one another by a dividing line or surface. The vortices are here not fully formed, but the surrounding substance pushes into the space created by the moving rod, first from one side and then from the other, making visible the strict rhythm of vortex formation. The boundary of this advance can be clearly seen as a kind of "joint" where "ball and socket" lie opposite one another. Closer observation reveals furthermore a delicate structure passing straight across this "joint". The accompanying simplified sketch of the same picture may help to make this clear.

An examination of joint formations in man and animal shows that the fine spongy bone structures in the ends of the bones run straight towards the surfaces of the joint and continue on the other side of the gap as though there were no interruption.

Even the solid bones solidify originally out of a liquid state; therefore it is understandable that in their inner structure the same

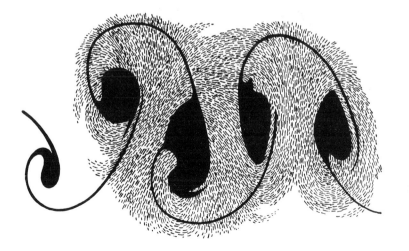

Absolute streamlines of the train of vortices in Plate 26

formations are found as in the vortex trains. In the one we see the structures in a state of flowing movement, in the other they are solidified into a fixed form, which then serves the flow of the static and dynamic forces in the limbs.

If water flows quickly over many small obstacles, such as pebbles, so many small trains of vortices are formed that they result in turbulence. Turbulence also arises if there is a great difference of speed in the water, say between the edge and the middle of a stream. The water is divided up by turbulence into countless circling inner surfaces. It is difficult to make the forms arising through turbulence clearly visible because the speeds are too great, but Plate 35 gives a rough impression of them.

Spongy bone structure in the human hip joint

The forms to be seen in the bark and grain of many kinds of wood are like solidified images of turbulent currents in water (Plates 34, 36, 38). Not that the actual movement of the liquids in the wood is turbulent; rather it is as though these formations were the mark left by the invisible streaming of currents and forces in the plants.

Plate 34 shows the arrangement of knots in the trunk of a cypress tree. Plate 38 shows the trunk of a mountain oak, and Plate 36 the grain in the trunk of an olive tree.

In the paired arrangement of the vortices in a vortex train we have a principle of construction which occurs in the formation of paired organs throughout the animal and human kingdom. It is

The bony structures in the nose of the deer are formed like vortices, whereby the inner surface is greatly enlarged (from v. Frisch)

above all in the fluid state that the fundamental principles of moving form in living development are revealed, principles which underlie physical creation in the bodies of animal and man. How these formative possibilities come to be present in water can only be understood through living nature and the spiritual creative forces behind it. In the embryo development of man and animal paired formations appear at the very early stage of the original segmentation. Many organs, for example limbs, kidneys and some of the sense organs, manifest this principle of formation.

A particularly clear picture of a train of vortices in solidified form can be found in the organs of smell of certain animals, as for example the deer. It is as though the bony structure had solidified out of the liquid state in the form of a train of vortices. Large surfaces are thus created, past which the air can stream, giving the animal its very acute sense of smell. (We shall see later that these formations are also appropriate to the laws of moving air.) The accompanying sketches are of a plane section; in reality we are of course dealing with three dimensional structures which have more in common with the type of form we shall be dealing with in the next chapter.

Enlarged detail of the bony structure in the nose of the deer

A train of vortices is caused by a twig or something dangling in the water and parting it. If a small rod is drawn across the surface of still water, the vortices arrange themselves in a rhythmical pattern where the water is parted. Similarly, where two streams meet, a train of vortices forms at the surface of contact. A particular form of vortex is caused when a very narrow stream flows into still water. Then a dividing surface flows between two masses of still water, and like all dividing surfaces it makes rhythmical formations. The vortices which thus arise spin in the opposite direction to those which arise when flowing water encounters an obstacle. These two types of formation—vortices which arise when flowing water encounters an obstacle or those that arise when a thin stream flows from a small opening into still water—are opposite to one another; the one is the reverse of the other. The law we have already mentioned is valid here too. With a narrow stream, small intervals occur between vortices, with a wide stream, large ones. Of course, if the stream is excessively wide only the surfaces of contact between the stream and the still water will curve rhythmically and curl round, and not the whole flowing stream.

So we may summarise with the following comparison, always assuming a constant speed of flow:

Narrow obstacle:

  many small vortices at short intervals.

Narrow stream:

  many small vortices at short intervals (Plate 24).

Wide obstacle:

  few large vortices at large intervals (Plate 26).

Wide stream:

  few large vortices at large intervals.[1]

Up to this point we have dealt with the rhythmical processes of vortex formation at the *surface* of the water. But trains of vortices are *three dimensional* formations. Every vortex is—as has been shown—a funnel of downward suction. We must imagine every train of vortices to be a rhythmical sequence of such funnels, of greater or lesser depth.

Comparison of two vortex trains from different causes: the direction in which vortices spin varies according to whether they are caused by an obstacle obstructing a stream of water or by a narrow stream of water entering still water through a small opening. The pattern of the vortices remains the same

Vortex funnel

---

[1] Strouhal's Law: $n \times \dfrac{d}{u} = $ const. $n = $ frequency, $d = $ thickness of rod, $u = $ speed.

Vortices can also be formed below the surface of the water; they are then somewhat modified but their formation can be easily understood on the basis of what has already been described. Two examples from the abundance of experimental possibilities, which can of course always be found in nature as well, are as follows:

1. A coloured stream flows below the surface into still water from a thin pipe with a rectangular section.
2. Flowing water encounters a wide submerged obstacle.

The stream from the pipe will describe in the still water a thin dividing surface, which becomes wavy and curls round. The form that arises (Plate 24) is very similar to that of a train of vortices on the surface of the water (Plate 28).

The water flowing round a wide obstacle will create a dividing surface along *all* submerged edges, that is along the whole outline of the obstacle, and this dividing surface, though itself consisting of water, will, like a sleeve, enclose an inner space. This dividing surface between an inner and an outer space undulates along its entire extent, contracting and expanding rhythmically. The expansions in the form of "bells" travel on beyond the obstacle with the current. A kind of pulsation is thus inscribed into the water as single quantities of water separate off, and the play of expansion and contraction becomes visible in the series of bell-like shapes (Plate 22). This expansion and contraction does not of course involve any increase or decrease in the density of the water. We nevertheless see how a pulsating rhythm is inscribed into the processes of flowing media. It arises as soon as currents meet under water, either in the wake of obstacles or when streams flow together from different directions.

To sum up we can say: behind a wide obstacle in flowing water a bell-shaped form arises, which is separated by a very clear dividing surface from the surrounding water, a form which itself consists of water and which travels onwards with the current. Something like an organic form is thus moulded in the uniform mass of the water, although there is absolutely no differentiation in substance. In other words we have here *the creation of form purely through movement*, inscribing itself into the water in rhythmical pulsation.

And now, instead of a constant stream from a submerged pipe, suppose only a short jet of liquid were to enter *still* water. It will form one single bell-like shape whose free edge curls outwards. As the bell travels, this edge rolls over further and further until the whole bell has turned inside out and curled into a ring (Plates 55–58). This rolling movement, which turns the form inside out, persists for a long time.

The ring consists of the most delicate spirally arranged lamelli, of which one can gain an impression by rolling up a cloth and then bending it round to form a ring. If this ring is now turned upon itself so that the layers at the inside move to the outside and then again to the inside, an approximate idea can be gained of the complicated pattern of movement in a ring that has arisen out of one of these "bells". As it travels the vortex-ring loses its circular form, and becomes "unstable" with excrescences on its circumference that make it look star-shaped (Plate 56). (The number of excrescences depends on the speed at which the original jet issues into the still water; a fast jet causes more bulges than a slow one.) The inner part of the ring has very complicated structures, which become partly visible if it collides with a flat surface held in its path. Experimentally this is possible for instance by letting the ring rise from below towards the surface of the water, with which it collides, scattering into a star-like shape (Plate 58). A similar thing happens when a drop falls into the surface of a liquid (Plate 59). This process can be used to demonstrate qualitative differences in liquids, for under the same conditions different fluids or liquid solutions will behave differently and produce varied star-like patterns.

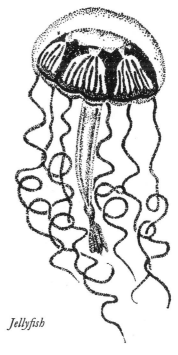

Jellyfish

By its pulsating method of propulsion the jellyfish causes mirror images of itself to arise in the water (diagrammatic sketch)

The process just described, when a jet of water moves into a still liquid, is not just an abstract idea, but can be found in the habits of many water creatures, for instance jellyfish. The jellyfish, a creature consisting of up to 99 per cent water, is itself an expression of the laws of movement in fluids. Even its outer shape is noticeably similar to vortex-bells, and so is its method of propulsion. The jellyfish progresses through the water by ejecting water from its body cavity, thus being driven forward by the backward thrust. Each jet of water takes on a bell-like shape, like the jellyfish itself but in reverse. It is like a mirror image of the jellyfish, moving in the opposite direction. With every jet of liquid it ejects, the jellyfish makes a mould of itself in the water, but only momentarily, for the form dissolves again. Repeating its jets, the jellyfish creates a whole sequence of bell-shaped forms, as though embodying a kind of "language" into the water, recreating itself again and again as a transient, fleeting form.

Particularly in the realm of jellyfish and medusae it is as though the water were to become partly independent, preparing a kind of "shell" for a sentient animal.

Many of the movements and forms we have already seen in water reappear as body and movement in the lower water animals. As well as jellyfish one need only think of sea-stars, sea-urchins, snails and many shells (Plates 42, 43).

"The resting state originates in movement"

> There is no doubt that our body is a moulded river.
> (Novalis, Aphorisms)

We have repeatedly seen how surfaces—both inner and outer ones —are very significant regions in the water, where rhythmical and formative processes take place. It is in the creation of surfaces, when an inner region is divided off from an outer one, that all structural formation comes about. This takes place through the interaction of the forces in both regions. In the following paragraphs we shall be turning our attention to this important principle.

Even a stone protruding from a stream gives rise to a definite formative boundary-surface in the water, which maintains itself as a stationary form in the midst of the streaming water.

As an obstacle in the stream, the stone offers resistance to the water flowing towards it. The water gives way on both sides and meets again a little further downstream. Behind the stone, downstream, a fairly calm backwater zone can be observed, separated by a clear dividing line (dividing surface) from the faster flowing water. This dividing surface is the result of the interaction of two forces: the force of the moving water and the force of resistance of the immobile, heavy stone. Two regions arise: an outer one, where the water is flowing past fairly fast, and an inner space in which the water flows more slowly, making manifold cross currents and circular motions.

Now let us imagine that we remove the stone, but maintain the force of resistance it makes against the current by sending in a stream of water from the place where it had lain. The following is a simplified description of an experiment along these lines. From the opening of a pipe in the bed of a stream or a canal, water enters the general current. It offers a resistance to the current, which has to give way. Thus, as before with the stone, a boundary surface arises which makes a *stationary* form within the water, surrounded by flowing liquid.—It is by no means only a solid obstacle in the path of a stream which creates a stationary form in the water. Such a form can come about through forces of movement in the midst of the flowing water itself. For example, a spring in its basin throws up from below a small circular mound of water. It gushes up out of the ground and then spreads out, being constantly replenished by new water. Similarly, in an artificial spring from a pipe in the ground water will surge up in a circular form, the force of the flow lessening as the water spreads away from the source. If there were a slope the water would all flow away in that one direction. Now if a direct current is made to flow over this spring, it will meet with resistance where the water of the spring comes up towards it. There will be a region where the forces of both streams balance each other out. Here, the water of the stream will not be able to penetrate the region of the spring nor will the spring water be able to push upstream. The oncoming water of the direct current avoids this meeting place and flows away sideways. Then, meeting the water flowing outwards from the spring, it is pushed out even further. The result of the interplay of the two currents is a boundary region, in which their

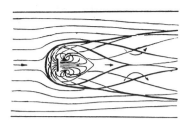

If water flows round a fixed plate, a dividing surface arises in the water (diagram after Kopp)

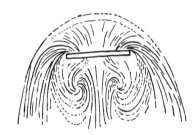

Stream-lines engraved by the water itself into the bed of a stream behind an obstructing plate (after Kopp)

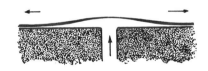

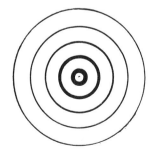

Diagram of a source, cross-section and seen from above

59

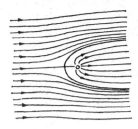

A dividing surface develops in the water between the flow of a direct current and a source

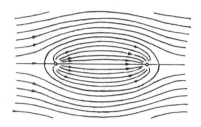

An enclosed dividing surface arises in the interplay of a source, a sink and a direct current

forces are held in balance. This boundary form simply indicates the moment of balance between the forces of the spring and those of the stream; it divides off the regions of the two currents according to their strength. If the spring grows stronger the boundary form opens out, if it weakens, the current of the stream overpowers the form and it shrinks. Dividing lines and surfaces of this kind are forms of balance between the forces of different regions; they respond with expanding and contracting movements as sensitively as do the scales of a balance to the smallest changes.

Now let us add to this arrangement a little further downstream a place where water is sucked away, for instance a drain pipe, making a "sink" in the bed of the canal. As was the case with the spring, the forces of suction from the "sink" will enter into relationship with the forces of the general current—but with the opposite effect, so that the boundary surface will close behind the outlet. In this way an enclosed inner space is divided off from an outer space. A small change in the size of the outlet will cause the boundary to expand or contract, so that the form as a whole becomes plumper or slimmer. It is easy to imagine that such boundary surfaces in flowing water are exceedingly delicate indicators of the smallest changes in the interplay of forces in the water. As quiescent forms they are the picture of these forces in the midst of the moving water and they react like the most delicate sense organs to any inner or outer change. Every source or sink added to this arrangement causes the form to bulge out or contract, and we see that the formative possibilities in such varying currents are infinite.

The outline of any figure can be created by the interplay of currents, surging outward, flowing parallel or contracting towards an outlet. On the other hand, the forms of any obstacles in a current of water have the same effect, though in reverse, as a corresponding system of sources and sinks by which they might be replaced. It is easy to imagine that the spiralling form of a vortex might also be used together with other currents to create quite specific boundary surfaces.

The boundary surface reacts like a sense organ to any change of pressure (change of speed) inside or outside the space enclosed by it. Isaachsen describes a case in point; water flows round a plate which acts as a dam, creating a backwater region, which is enclosed by a sensitive boundary surface. He says, "It is as though in the backwater there is an organ, which measures and regulates the pressure, and this is indeed the case. . . . The tip of the backwater is the "feeler", the organ that measures and regulates, constantly registering the pressure of the speed of flow."

So boundary surfaces arise through the confluence of currents from different directions and picture the states of balance of the forces at work in water. They can make enclosed forms which lie *quiescent* amid *flowing* movement and respond with expansion or contraction to any delicate change in the currents. They really are like delicate sense organs.

Water flowing round an obstructing plate or slab (after Isaachsen)

Is it not a striking phenomenon that in the midst of flowing movement forms arise, not through any differentiation in substance, but simply through the interplay of currents and their forces? This points to a formative principle based on the interplay of movements rather than on material substance. It is movement that takes hold of the substance and moulds it. Only through a true observation of these facts is it possible to approach an understanding of the processes which lead to the creation of forms in the embryo; neither in matter alone, nor in the process of cell-division is there a basis for understanding what is happening in this sphere.

Flowing processes are active in the growth of all organisms. Through faster growth some parts protrude, others are held back through a suspension of growth or even dissolved again. In all stages of embryonic development there is an interplay between forces of welling outflow and suctional inflow, by which the respective shapes arise. We see it in the very first stages of embryonic development; the swelling enlargement of the fertilised ovum and the subsequent intucking in gastrulation.[1] In the course of the

[1] From what has been said it will be clear that we are concerned here with a general principle of formation, and are not considering the differences in the embryonic development of the various species.

development of the embryo these principles, acting as formative processes, can be found again and again. They are superior to, and regulate the mere division of cells. But even this superior principle of outflow and inflow, with its streaming movements and temporal sequences, is in its turn the tool of the creative idea that lies behind it. We come across this principle in all conceivable variations in embryonic development. A multitude of sources, sinks and currents work together to create the living form. This interplay is like the diversity of an orchestra with its instruments, that have their entries and their rests and are moulded into a *single* "body of sound" by an invisible conductor according to a strictly systematic score. Often outflowing currents are active—for instance when the optic vesicle is formed—which, after a time cease and pass on the theme to another part of the development. The score and its entries remain of course in a region superior to this process, from which they penetrate the impressionable liquid substance and cause it to take on a harmonious form.

A *universal* and *harmonious* concord of all possibilities will bring forth the human form. Emphasis on the development of certain details will lead rather to animal formations with their specialised one-sidedness. One may think for instance of the immoderate protuberance of the bill of a crane compared with the moderate proportions of the mouth of the human being. But of course it is just such one-sided features that bring to expression the nature of the respective animals. (See *Man and Animal*, by Poppelbaum.)

We shall not go generally into the details of embryology, assuming that they are common knowledge, but restrict ourselves to one example, the development of the eye, in which such varying movements work together to form a sense organ.

First the small bulge of the optic vesicle grows out of the forebrain. The optic vesicle touches the ectoderm from the inside and this in turn becomes invaginated at this point towards the optic vesicle and

The development of the human eye

thickens to form the lense. The optic vesicle is squashed in by it and becomes cupped around it. The lense—moving inwards—then loses contact with the surface and becomes enclosed by the newly formed optic cup.

It can also be seen how the retina in the human being has arisen out of the principles of source and sink. The point where the optic nerve leaves the eye is like the outlet—the sink—in a stream of water, and the neighbouring *fovea centralis* like a spring. The way the two work together is clearly recognisable in the diagram of the "field of forces" of the nerve fibres in the retina.

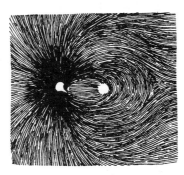

Nerve fibres in the retina around the fovea centralis and the point of exit of the optic nerve (after v. Michel)

Even in water the surfaces of the forms that are created by flowing movements are unbelievably sensitive. But it is a sensitivity which is not based on any nervous system, which arises purely out of the interplay of forces and is not to be understood from the aspect of the substance. How delicate then must a skin be, which constitutes a boundary surface which is also differentiated in substance! Surely here Nature reveals one of her secrets by anticipating sensitivity in flowing movement without needing a nervous system! Does she not actually incorporate in the substance of the nerve-sense organs in living creatures the sensitivity already present as a function in fluids? At a primitive level the amoeba, with the sensitive surface of its body, is an example of the principles of source and sink. It does not solidify into a fixed form but remains in the flowing, constantly changing fluid state of embryonic processes. At will it can thrust out a limb, now here, now there, by pushing out its watery body, retracting it again by suction and thrusting it out again elsewhere. It responds to every stimulation from outside through a change in its surface form. It either flows towards the source of stimulation, thrusting out a limb of its body liquid in this direction, or it retreats,

An amoeba "engulfs" and absorbs its prey

63

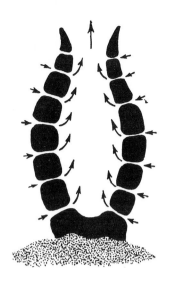

Currents of outflow and inflow as water passes through a sponge (after Kühn)

drawing its body liquid away. Here is a first gentle hint of how animal instinct expresses itself simply in living, flowing substance.

The most varied versions of these possibilities may be found among the unicellular water animals. For instance some creatures are able to thrust out a limb and fix it for a while and later to transform it back into a liquid state again. They can make free use of the delicate change from gel to sol, making the form of their bodies changeable or permanent. Indeed, they revel in their true element in this unstable, sensitive "border region".

Other creatures mould their bodies as though to form only the shell for these processes of sink and source. With the sponge, water streams into the inside through narrow channels on the surface (sink). This water collects in the centre of the creature and passes out again in a concentrated stream, like a spring. In the course of this process the particles of food in the water are absorbed. The stronger the stream issuing forth, the stronger the suction (sink) inwards, and vice versa. The visible form of the sponge grows out of the relationship between the two.

The most simple form of spring, one with a pulsating activity, has already been described in connection with the jellyfish. This creature ejects a rhythmical series of jets into the surrounding water, imprinting its own image upon the water. The form of the jellyfish is no more than an expression of the simple pulsating movement in a spring, transformed through the resistance of the surrounding water. All these are archetypal, creative movements, working in accord; they have been described separately simply for the sake of greater clarity. But Nature does reveal her secrets at particular moments; some of her archetypal movements she reveals separately by densifying them to clothe a living creature.

And if Nature creates creatures in which she reveals *one* of her creative movements, she also creates *one* living creature in whom all archetypal movements stream together: the human being. . . . "The human being as we see him is a completed form. But this form has been created out of movement. It has arisen from those primeval forms which were continually taking shape and passing away again. Movement does not proceed from quiescence; on the contrary, that which is in a state of rest originates in movement." (From a lecture given by Rudolf Steiner on 24th June, 1924.)

Water, Nature's Sense Organ

The formative boundary surfaces in flowing movement prove to be areas of sensitivity. They respond to the slightest changes in their surroundings by expanding, contracting or making rhythmical waves. Water creates an infinite variety of these surfaces and is therefore not merely an inert mass, as we usually think. It is interwoven with countless sensitive membranes, which are prepared to perceive everything taking place in the surroundings. Water is not enclosed within its inner surfaces but open to its surroundings and to all the stimuli and formative impulses from without. It is the impressionable medium *par excellence*. Indeed it is so sensitive that not only does it react to changes in its immediate surroundings, but also to the delicate, imponderable influences of the planetary universe. This may seem an exceedingly bold statement. But experiments in this field show that water really is capable of reacting to the delicate influences resulting from changes in the cosmos.

For instance, water shaken in a vessel can be caused to move in such a way that the inner surfaces thus created all slide past each other in the moving liquid. As soon as the movement ceases, the formation of inner surfaces, and thus also the great impressionability, is arrested, and the "sense organ" closes itself. If water is shaken in this way, all the many forms of movement arise in it which we have been describing singly for the sake of clarity. The same is true of the natural movement of water, in which also a great variety of movements combine. Not only the shaking of a container but also other kinds of movement can open up the water as a sense organ.

As a striking example among the abundance of constellations in the heavens we will choose an experiment made on the day of a total eclipse of the sun.

During the course of the day at regular intervals—say every quarter of an hour—a different vessel filled with water is shaken rhythmically for a short time. Each time this is done a kind of sense organ, which closes again when the movement ceases, is opened to the momentary happenings in the heavens. And each time a somewhat different situation in the universe is imprinted upon the water: the gradual movement of the moon towards the sun, the commencement of the eclipse, the totality of the eclipse and the gradual movement of the moon away from the sun. At the end of a series of experiments like this the whole course of the happenings of the day is contained in the row of bottles that have been shaken. How can this be made visible? There are various methods, of which we have chosen the following: in the water of each vessel grains of wheat are caused to germinate; this can be done days or even weeks later, as long as the water has not meanwhile been disturbed anew. The grains of wheat are all placed in the water at the same time and under the same external conditions; the effect of the impressions which permeate the water will be seen in the growth of the blades. During the same span of time the blade in the water of one vessel will grow better than that in another. The lengths of the different blades in the different vessels will depict the course of the eclipse. The blades in the water

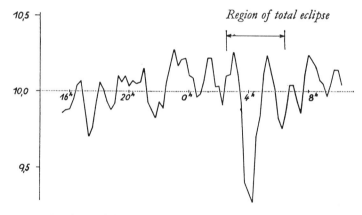

An eclipse of the sun is imprinted on moving water (graph of plant growth)

shaken at the time of the total eclipse do not grow as high as those in water shaken before or after. A graph can be made of the lengths of the blades in the consecutive samples of water and the so-called growth curve results. Other planetary constellations will give growth curves of a different character.[1]

---

[1] Mathematically interested readers may be assured that the result of the experiment satisfies strict statistical requirements. More information about these experiments may be found in the author's book *Grundlagen der Potenzforschung*.

Apart from the method described above, experiments were also carried out using the method of capillary dynamolysis evolved by L. Kolisko. The results here too showed that the quality of the water changes according to the time (constellation) at which it is shaken. Of course the impressions are lost as soon as the water is shaken anew, because it is then opened again to the cosmic influences of the moment. What significance does this have in the great realm of nature?

A stream, bubbling merrily over the stones, forms countless inner surfaces and tiny vortices, which are all sense organs open to the cosmos, and which perceive the course of events in the heavens. Water passes on the "impressions" it has received wherever it is absorbed by the earth and the plants, by the animals and man. In moving water the earthly world thus allows the ever changing life in the universe of the stars to flow into the course of its own life.

Water covers the greater part of the earth's surface and is continually in the most varied motion. There is such unlimited movement in this sheath of water encompassing the earth that it can on a global scale even be regarded as an organ mediating between earth and cosmos, integrating the earth into the course of cosmic events and enabling it to take part in these events.

Is it not of great significance that the world of the stars permeates all movements of water, that water infuses all earthly life with the events of the cosmos, that all life processes are through water intimately connected with the course of the stars? Wherever there is moving water—in the trickling stream, in the rolling river, in the rhythmical ebb and flow of the waves, in the foam of the breakers—everywhere it is illumined by the world of the stars. Thus water becomes an image of the stream of time itself, permeated with the rhythms of the starry world. All the creatures of the earth live in this stream of time, it flows within them, and, as long as it flows, sustains them in the stream of life.

Cosmic events and water are linked with the stream of time in the ebb and flow of the tides—in high tide and low tide. The connection between the course of the moon and the tides is so obvious and well known that we need not go into it in detail here.

On a smaller scale, too, the rhythms of the moon pulsate in the water. In olden times these rhythms were taken into account when wells were dug. This was usually done only during certain phases of the moon and when it was in certain positions in the zodiac. Even within the earth, water rises and falls with the course of the moon. When the moon is in certain positions, water is soon reached, but it also dries up again more easily. At other times it is necessary to dig deeper in order to reach the water, but it then remains constant. Recent observations in deserted and flooded mines show how the subterranean water reservoirs are influenced by the rhythms of the moon.

Traditional customs among lumbermen, to the effect that the rivers spread out at full moon and burrow in the depths at new moon, show that the forms of movement within the water obviously have a particular connection with the course of the moon and its phases. Accordingly, in naturally flowing rivers, it is difficult to float the logs at full moon, as they are washed up on the banks, whereas at new moon they are drawn into the middle of the waterway and are thus easier to control. It is gradually becoming evident that observations like this from everyday *experience* in the past are not to be put aside lightly.

To mention only one example. It is well known that a large amount of pebbles and detritus sometimes collects in the water of a river dammed up to supply a power station, and has to be removed at great expense. It is however possible to make use of the experience that if the sluices are opened at certain phases and positions of the moon, the water itself has the power to wash away the debris.

Customs still practised today sometimes indicate knowledge of the change of the quality of water brought about by certain constellations in the heavens. For instance in some districts of the Himalayas where knowledge of this kind is still cultivated, all water containers in the houses must be emptied before or after an eclipse.

Lumbermen reckon with the change in the stream of sap during the year. The stream of sap in the trees varies according to the phases of the moon and its position in the zodiac, and so accordingly does the durability and quality of the timber. Timber felled at new moon in winter is the most durable. To this day in South America valuable hardwoods are stamped with marks indicating the phase of the moon at which they were felled. Their commercial value is determined accordingly!

Many examples could be taken from the world of living creatures to demonstrate the connection between water and the course of the stars, but we shall let one speak for all and simply ask: is it not remarkable, that water animals actually know how to make use of the processes in the heavens? A certain kind of smelt, distantly related to the salmon, inhabit the open sea. Once a year at their spawning time in May they approach the coast of California. They wait near the shore until the tide reaches its highest point on the third day after full moon and allow themselves to be carried up on to the beach by the *last*, highest wave. There the females lay their eggs in the wet sand and the males fertilise them, and with the next wave they return again to the open sea. But this wave is already the first of the receding tide. So the eggs on the sand are left untouched by the water and not swept away, for this wave does not reach them on the beach. The high tides in the following thirteen days do not again attain this level. Not until fourteen days later is the tide again high enough to reach the spawn of the smelt; it hatches only a few minutes before being washed out to sea, not to return to the shore until years later, fully grown, for a moment on this third day after full moon in May. These fish live in such close connection with the cosmic movements of the water—for that is what the tides are—that they "know" with astronomical exactitude to the second when the tide has reached its highest point on the third day after full moon in May. Only for one moment in the year are the relative positions of sun, moon and earth suitable for them.

So the world of moving water absorbs the constellations of the stars in the heavens and passes them on to the earth and its creatures. Cosmic events, the world of water and the living creatures in it form a totality. The latter, as water creatures, simply make visible the cosmic events that live and move in their element. Creatures living on dry land also have part in these events through the circulation of liquids in them.

Through the rhythm of breathing, the laws of the cosmic world penetrate the beat of the heart and the streaming of the liquid blood in the human being. A man draws breath eighteen times a minute, 25,920 times a day, and is thus connected in his respiratory system with the course of the sun, for it takes as many years for the vernal equinox to have moved through the great circle of the zodiac. On the other hand the breathing of the human being is in a ratio of 1 : 4 with the circulation of the liquid blood, as there are seventy-two beats of the pulse for every eighteen breaths drawn. This relationship between air and water (blood) would not appear to be accidental, for it comes again in nature outside man. The speed of propagation of sound is four times faster in water than in air. The relationship is particularly close in the case of sea water, which because of its qualities has often been compared with the blood of the human being. So there is a path that leads from the rhythms of the macrocosm via the breathing of the human being to the processes of his blood circulation. The same cosmic order, reflected in these number ratios, permeates the universe and man.

We have demonstrated the ability of water to take part in cosmic processes. Let us now consider the well-known phenomenon in water usually referred to as the Principle of Archimedes.

It is well known that a heavy stone lifted from the bed of a river suddenly seems still heavier when lifted out of the water. It seems to weigh less in the water than outside it. It is therefore said that as a submerged body it is subject to upthrust. How does this arise? If a stone falls to the ground it is pulled downward by a force that one must imagine to be drawing at the centre of gravity of the stone. It usually falls vertically downwards. This is of course also true of every drop of water. A submerged body however makes it obvious that within the water there are also other forces, which not only work downward but *from all sides*. The weight of the water presses vertically at every point of the submerged body. The force at each point is as great as the weight of the pillar of water above it. Thus the pressure on the undersurface is greater than at any other part.

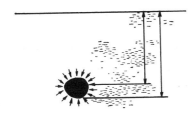

The pressure of the water is always vertical to the surface of a submerged body. The pressure from underneath is greater than that from above, hence the upthrust of Archimedes' Principle

Therefore of course the weight of the submerged body is diminished and it receives an upthrust which corresponds to the weight of the volume of water displaced by it. In opposition to the force of gravity which always pulls downwards, there is in the water a principle that can be said to work from all sides. Forces from all sides, from the surroundings, act upon the submerged body, and it thereby loses weight. Water, by allowing its own forces of weight to work upon a body from all sides, thus making it lighter, aligns itself with cosmic forces working in from the universe. It places itself in the centre between the forces working from the stars and those emanating from the earth.

This ability of water to make bodies lighter through the forces of upthrust and to lift them towards the starry spheres, is of great significance for all life on earth. All plant growth would be inconceivable without this propensity of water. Its power for example to rise up 80 yards or more in an American pine tree demonstrates most impressively its ability to overcome the force of gravity. Everywhere in nature it places itself as mediator between earth and cosmos, redeeming solid bodies from their weight and maintaining the connection between cosmic events and the earth.

In what follows we shall call the forces raying in from the world of the stars, from the universe surrounding us, universal forces and turn to ideas first put forward in this connection by Rudolf Steiner. There is a polarity between two opposites: centric, gravitational forces which work on the centres of gravity of objects and are measurable in terms of weight; and universal forces, flowing in from the whole sphere of the heavens, causing lightness.

Water, as mediator between the centric and the universal forces, setting them in balance and interweaving them with its very substance, reveals the activity of the heavens on earth.

The forces of upthrust—we may also use the word "levity" as opposed to gravity—represent a quality in water without which the life of the earth would be inconceivable. Water further emphasises this quality through its behaviour with relation to warmth and cold. When frozen it becomes as hard as a stone and is subject to the laws of gravity, but it immediately escapes again from these laws because as ice it becomes lighter than liquid water. It is well known that ice floats on water. If this were not so, if ice were to become heavier than water and sink, then the oceans and all the water basins of the earth would gradually fill with ice from the bottom upwards and the earth would be transformed into a frozen waste. But by floating as ice, water once again reveals that it is its nature to serve life. Its density is greatest at a temperature of 4°C., i.e. above freezing point. At the temperature of 4°C. it is most concentrated, below and above this temperature it expands again, thus also becoming lighter per unit volume. Water that has seeped into the nooks and crannies of the cliffs expands as it freezes, thus cracking the hardest rocks. In this way it starts off the dead, hard element on the way back to life. As through the action of water in the course of time the rocks crumble to a finer and finer consistency, they become the basis for plant growth and are again received into the great cycle of living nature. The same takes place each year in the fields, where the freezing of the earth and its organic components helps to prepare the fertile sod. This process is supported by the propensity of water to dissolve solid substances, to which, among other things, its great purifying property is due. Only through this ability to dissolve substances can it become a medium of transport for nourishment to and within organisms. We need only remember how apparently effortlessly water can dissolve a lump of sugar, which it would cost us a certain amount of effort to crack to pieces. On the other hand it is even possible for water to absorb gaseous substances, for instance carbonic acid, whereby it increases its ability to attack what is solid. Under suitable conditions it can of course deposit the substances it has dissolved, creating for instance such interesting formations as the sinter terraces in the Yellowstone National Park in North America (aragonite formations).

The dead rock is brought back to life not only through the ability of water to burst asunder and dissolve substances, but also through its mechanical properties, among which upthrust or buoyancy is one of the most important. The rock split off the mountain side rolls down the scree slopes and finally reaches the river where it loses some of its weight and is rolled on further. As though in a great mill the water smooths all its edges and corners, grinding it against other stones and rolling it onwards in glacial pot-holes or along the bed of a stream, till it is finally reduced to pebbles or sand and the finest particles, which further downstream form the basis of fruitful arable land. The great culture of Ancient Egypt would have been inconceivable without this process. Religious rites accompanied the arrival of the Nile floods and the irrigation of the land, for every year the fertile mud—the foundation of the land between the deserts—was washed down anew.

The incurved forms of a glacial pot-hole are caused by the grinding movement of stones driven round and round by the water

Is it not characteristic of an element that everywhere serves life, that it rounds off sharp edges and all too solid forms, grinding them down and making them accessible to life? Indeed it even gives the stones in their shapes a similarity to living organs, creating here also spherical or elliptical forms. Particularly impressive are the stone balls in glacial pot-holes, milling and grinding the hard rock into round and hollow forms (Plate 49).

All these processes take place simultaneously in rhythmical repetition. It is the rhythm that proves stronger than rigidity. Year in, year out, it splits the rocks, again and again the rubble is ground down by rhythmically recurring flood waters; every wave, every tiny trickle of water is rhythmically active in this crumbling process; century by century the stones roll rhythmically in the glacial pot-holes, grinding the rock as in a great mortar. Every river bed resembles a series of these pot-holes, in which the river delves down into the hard subsoil. Shallows alternate with deep pools, which at times of flood are hollowed out more and more by the rolling stones and the might of the current.—At the same time the river uses the detritus that it has ground up for itself for the construction of its river bed. It builds up its own shores, sorting out the coarser and finer detritus and setting it down in banks. It is an important quality of water that it has not only destructive forces, in the usual sense of the word, i.e. splitting and grinding forces, but that with the help of these forces it creates its own limitations, using them to build its banks or even to place obstacles in the way of its own torrent. It is very important to recognize this upbuilding quality of the water; it is its own compensation for its forces of destruction. Water destroys the hard rock and thus slowly brings it to life, but at the same time it tames its own surplus energy with what it has destroyed. The detritus and other materials, constantly on the move, are again and again deposited in the form of barriers and obstacles in the way of the rushing torrent. These obstacles are often found at fairly regular, rhythmical intervals. Deep reaches alternate with shallows where the speed of the current is checked. What it means to the whole aspect of the countryside when the water of a river is slowed down on its course, becomes obvious when compared with the opposite picture—canalisation, of which the disastrous effects are well known.[1]

An impressive picture of the way in which a river builds its own barriers is offered by the Plitvice lakes in Yugoslavia, which arise because the calcium deposited by the water forms barriers across the current at regular intervals. In this way the river is slowed down and dammed up to form separate lakes.

The Mississippi at its mouth in the Gulf of Mexico is an example of how a great river builds its own banks. The river deposits the fine material with which it is laden into the sea, piling it up till it reaches water level, thus extending the banks out into the sea. During the course of a long time the Mississippi has washed down so much firm ground, that today cities stand where once there was nothing but the sea. In a river system such as this a prevailing unity is evident; the separate branches of the river all belong to a great organism. The Mississippi and its tributaries form a totality of this kind.

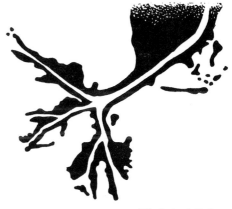

Mississippi Delta

Every river has its catchment area with tributaries, which in their turn have lesser tributaries and these again yet smaller ones. If the latter are traced to their source, they are found to lose themselves beyond their springs in a network of capillary veins, which are often made visible by being filled out with a matted tangle of plant roots. This system of a river in its catchment basin is like a network

[1] What has been said does not exclude the fact that it may be necessary in moderation to correct the course of a river and incorporate it into the cultivated countryside.

of veins. Further downstream the main artery unites with a still greater one; for instance the Neckar flows into the Rhine, of which it is only a tributary. In this way all the different river systems unite to form one great network over the face of the earth, comparable to

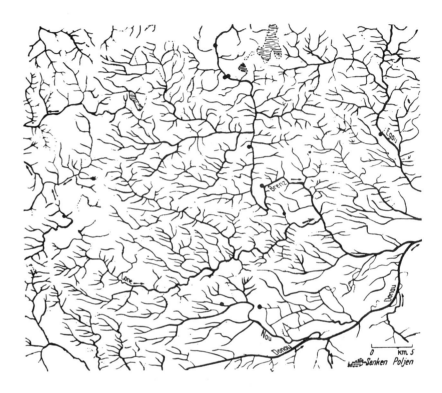

Network of water veins in the catchment basin of the Brenz, a tributary of the upper Danube (after G. Wagner)

the network of veins in the human being. In man, too, the blood vessels of the separate organs unite to form a totality. The blood of the human being even builds its own "banks", in the form of vessels, out of the blood corpuscles in suspension in it.

In the circulatory system of the human being, where every change or injury is noticed, the circulation as a whole accommodates itself to any disturbance; in a similar way the veins of a river system "perceive" any change in the network, though this perception may not immediately become apparent to the human observer. The river system will eventually, for good or for evil, accommodate itself to any such changes. A sad example of this is the ill-considered straightening of the upper reaches of a river, which can lead to severe flooding in the lower reaches. This can change the form of a healthy river right down to its ground-water reserves and its subterranean capillary system. Not only are the lower reaches of the rivers affected by such alterations but also the land upstream. The fine network of water veins in the ground changes completely in the banks on both sides of a river which has been straightened and it digs deeper and deeper into the ground. Rivers thus deepened drain away the surrounding water, sucking it away from a wider and wider area, which is then in great danger of becoming arid.

Flowing water always attempts to form networks. This may be seen where the sea is shallow when the receding tide leaves deep veins in the sand (Plates 10, 17). Even in detail this network of channels in the sand reveals the curving meander-formation which, as we have seen, is one of the archetypal movements of water.

In the conflict of water with the solid earth, not only its dissolving and grinding activity must be taken into account, but also its ability to deposit and arrange substances. We have already mentioned this activity in connection with shingle and sandbanks, and while discussing the way in which it builds its own banks and creates such formations as the sinter terraces. This also is always a rhythmical activity. On a large scale it is evident in the barriers or deposits that water again and again places in its own path in rhythmical sequence; on a small scale it occurs in the repeated formation of ripple marks on the sandy beds of rivers or on the sea shore. The material deposited is constantly being rhythmically moulded and formed. Like the large barriers, these ridges, too, often lie across the current. Their form varies according to the depth and speed of the water and the kind of material being deposited. The play of forms in these ripple marks is very varied. Examples are given in Plates 8 and 12. Closer observation will show that these ridge formations are constantly changing, and slowly being pushed forward to make room for new material. Their progress is much slower than that of the water flowing over them; two different movements take place simultaneously. The more rapidly flowing water imprints a slower movement on to the material below it, forming it at the same time; whole landscapes in miniature, with gently sloping hills, ravines and so on, are imprinted on the plastic foundation. Again and again curved and spiralling surfaces arise, like those with which we are already familiar. We are again reminded of organic formative processes, according to which for instance the muscles in the higher animals and man are formed (Plate 18).

These formative processes in the water take place according to laws similar to those which prevail in the forming of solid bones;

vertebral and rib forms are indeed "deposits" of the liquid element. Some of the organic formative processes in man and animal may be found again, in the movements of water—the "blood of the earth" —and the way it meets with the solid element (Plates 9, 18).

Rhythmical patterns of ridges also arise in stationary water, when ripples move over the surface. This occurs even in small dimensions if there is a sufficiently fine substance on the bottom, for example, a deposit of lime in the bottom of a jar.

To sum up: water flows and streams on the earth as ceaselessly as the stream of time itself. It is the fundamental melody that forever accompanies life in all its variations. Unremittingly it belabours the solid earth, grinding, milling, destroying, levelling out, and at the same time elsewhere building up again, creating anew, preparing for life. As the life blood of the earth, in the great network of veins, it shifts unbelievable amounts of substance, which everywhere accompany the life processes of the earth and its creatures. In a ceaseless process it transforms the hardest rocks and the highest mountains into a flowing, finely ground stream of substance, and it dissolves finished forms, preparing them for new creation. Water is thus the great exchanger and transformer of substances in all forms of metabolism. Constantly dissolving and solidifying, washing away and re-forming, in perpetual transformation, water is ever-lastingly creating the organism of the earth planet. Is it not as though the stream of time itself becomes visible to physical eyes in this perpetual activity of water? Water always proves stronger than anything too solidly anchored in space, continually leading it back into the stream of time, of living development.

In the passage of the earth round the sun, the stream of time divides itself rhythmically into years and days, through the rhythms of the moon and the planets. So, too, the waters of the earth rhythmically work upon the material world.

The objection could be raised that all this happens quite automatic-ally according to the fixed rules of cause and effect. But in these processes cause and effect so very often change places. In many processes in the realm of the liquid element the cause is in the same moment also effect and the effect at the same moment cause, where-by they unite in manifold interplay to form a moving totality. Just as in a living organism cause and effect intermingle in a simultaneous correlation, so do they also in water. For instance, the waves flowing over the beach arrange the sand in ridges, but at the same time these formations affect the waves and influence their forms. An interplay like this resembles an intimate co-operation which results in the creation of a third factor, which, however, can only be seen from a higher level, when the human mind apprehends the prevailing whole.

The creatures of nature can also only be understood from this higher level. In them Nature reveals her secrets. The wise, instinctive actions of the animals speak of the wisdom of nature creative in all the elements. Water checks its rapid torrent by placing barriers in its own way; it slows down its course and remains in a healthy relationship with the surrounding countryside. By flowing more slowly it prevents the fruitful earth from being washed out to sea and gives it back to the land by depositing it again. A creature like the beaver is really like the embodiment of all this wisdom. In all its actions it unites itself with the propensity of water to regulate its own flow, thus increasing the fruitfulness of the land. The beaver brings this activity of the water to still greater perfection; by constructing dams it slows down the flow of the water and regulates it. Its instinctive actions are so bound up in what is happening between water and the countryside that it forestalls a flood by raising its dams, thus preventing destruction. For instance, the renowned fruitfulness of the earth of the Mississippi basin is considered to be the result of the activities of the beavers over thousands of years, who by damming the river slowed it down, thus causing the fertile mud to be deposited. The desperate efforts to reintroduce beavers to the upper reaches of the river, where they have been exterminated, testifies to the importance which today is once again being attached to them. They are an important counter measure to the straightening of the rivers and streams by which inconceivable amounts of the most fruitful earth are annually washed down into the sea.

Three characteristic features of water, forming together a complete picture, emerge from our considerations hitherto. Two of these are clear for all to see, the third is almost unknown, requiring very sensitive methods of observation. The first is the activity of water in all metabolic processes in the great organism of the earth and in each separate living creature. The second is its close connection with all rhythmical processes in time and space. The third comes to light in our observation of the sensitivity of boundary surfaces, indicating that water is a cosmic sense organ of the earth. All three functions—functions which are well known to us in the world of living organisms—form a whole.

Is it not as though water were itself an organism? Do we not see in water the threefold organism of man himself—an archetypal picture, though purely functional, of the metabolic, nerve-sense and rhythmic organisations?[1] Perhaps these three characteristics of water form the basis of *all* living organisms, whose specialization goes in the direction of one or other of these three characteristics? Let us now consider the three characteristics in the light of this new question, commencing with water as a "substance".

As all organisms consist chiefly of water, it is obvious that water is the primary and most essential element for all living processes. It refrains from taking on a form of its own, but fills out any form offered it and envelops any which dip into it. In their development many creatures, including man himself, climb out, as it were, from the water on to dry land. The human being, enveloped in the maternal organism and entirely floating in water, gradually creates the distinct form of his organs out of the liquid. In the second month he still consists almost entirely of water, and even as an old man about 60 per cent of his substance is water. The first and very often the last nourishment taken by a human being is liquid substance. It is only because water flows and dissolves substances that organisms —plant, animal and man—can take solid substance as nourishment at all. The whole process of breaking down and building up of substances within an organism is unthinkable without water; by far the greater proportion of chemical changes is dependent on water as a

[1] See the basic explanations by Rudolf Steiner in "Riddles of the Soul".

mediating and dissolving element. In its own nature, water does not commit itself in any way; chemically it is neutral and therefore has a multitude of possibilities for nearly all chemical changes.[1]

In metabolism, however, it is not merely a question of transformation of substances, but also of the accompanying heat processes; for these too, water is the basis. It is able to absorb not only large quantities of dissolved substances but also a great amount of heat and to transport it wherever it goes. The countries of northern Europe owe their mild climate to this fact; the Gulf Stream flowing past them brings the warmth of the tropics with which it is laden. It flows on into polar regions, where eventually, much cooled, it densifies and sinks to the bottom, still flowing on further and beginning a circulation which fills the Atlantic Ocean to the depths, causing a great process of oceanic "metabolism". (There are similar processes in the Pacific.) Ocean currents of this kind play an important part in the fluctuating temperatures of the earth planet; they belong to the great regulatory systems of the climates, on which the life of the earth depends, which are adjusted down to fractions of a degree Centigrade, e.g. in the average yearly temperature. Thus our attention is drawn to the ability of water to absorb large quantities of heat. This also plays an important part in the blood of the human being.

A gramme of water takes into itself eighty calories when it changes from ice to water of a temperature of 0°C., and each further increase of a degree in temperature means taking in a further calory per gramme of water. This is of course approximate; a more detailed observation shows that the amount of heat needed to increase the temperature by one degree is not the same over the whole range of the thermometer, and that a minimum amount is needed around 37°C. At this temperature—which is the temperature of human blood—water is most easily warmed. May we not look here for a relationship with man? Does not water reflect, as though in anticipation, the laws of man's warmth organism? In any case the unique properties of water in connection with warmth are fundamental to the human organism. We may indeed discuss all the questions concerning water's relation to heat not only from the aspect of water, but also from the point of view of man.

[1] L. J. Henderson's basic work "Die Umwelt des Lebens" gives information on the important processes of osmosis and diffusion within the living cell.

Whichever material qualities of water we study, they all point to the world of living organisms with their metabolic processes, to man himself, and finally far beyond him.

The third of the above mentioned qualities of water, its sensitivity, is the opposite of the metabolic process. Even as a substance, in the liquid state, it is in the nature of water to be sensitive to the smallest stimuli, which results in effects that can be clearly observed. A slight rise in temperature, for instance, will at once considerably change its fluidity. Its fluidity, the state of being easily displaced, is at every moment an expression of the conditions of warmth in its surroundings. Just as honey flows more easily in the warm, so does water when it is warmed; sun-lit water is less dense and forms vortices more easily than that of a shady forest stream. When it leaves the dark spring or the cool woods it adjusts itself even in its inmost "structure" to the new conditions. It opens itself like a sense organ to outer influences. In face of the light it becomes, through its qualities of reflection and transparency, like an eye for the whole earth.

In surface tension, through which water strives to attain a spherical, drop form, it again shows great sensitivity towards the influences of its surroundings. The merest traces of substances added to water suffice to cause a quick and considerable change in its surface tension. The surface tension of water that has stood for a few moments is considerably different from that of fresh water. In the same way it reacts sensitively to the most minute changes in temperature. The surface tension of a jet of liquid issuing from a thin pipe is just like an instrument, played upon above all by the rhythmical processes of the surroundings. For instance a jet of liquid issuing from an opening disintegrates in the rhythm of approaching sound waves into separate drops; or it reacts in a corresponding manner to the most minute changes in the surrounding electrical conditions. Water's "sensitivity" is as great as that of the human ear. A gentle breeze blowing over the surface of water immediately creases the surface into the tiniest capillary waves, but also any small rod drawn through water, or obstructing flowing water, immediately causes it to react with a whole system of surface tension waves (Plate 6). Water may be even more "impressed" by a stone thrown into it, and it passes this impression on rhythmically to its whole mass. The great rhythms of the tides are a response to forces which work in the interplay of earth and cosmos . . . and for which, through its great impressionability, the element of water is a receptive "sense organ".

As we have shown in the experiments already described, the inner surfaces permeating the whole mass of flowing water really act like sensory membranes by which the water is susceptible to delicate influences from the distant surroundings of the earth.

The boundary surfaces arising in the interplay of different streams resemble such membranes, responding immediately with expansion or contraction to the most delicate changes in the forces causing them. We described them as sensitive forms of balance, on which it is possible for the most delicate influences to play. Isaachsen describes these boundary surfaces, arising from the interplay of different forces, as "feelers", comparing them to instruments with the sensitivity of sense organs, and Novalis calls the element of water simply the "sensitive chaos".

Every activity of water takes place rhythmically; this is the second of the characteristics mentioned above. Every influence on the surface of a stretch of water immediately calls forth a rhythmical series of waves; every twig dangling in a river causes a train of vortices in rhythmical sequence; about every surface of contact between two streams there is a rhythmical play of waves and vortices. The interplay of earth, moon and sun finds its immediately visible expression in the rhythmical waves of the tides. A rhythm as great as that of the advancing and receding tides can become the bearer of countless smaller rhythms, for instance of the waves caused by the wind, hurrying across its surface. But there must always be an interplay between at least two forces in order to create a balancing rhythm between them. Water is the element which brings about a state of balance everywhere. Even within itself it maintains a harmony between its qualities as an earthly substance and its cosmic aspect of sensitivity. Rhythm is simply its "life element", and the more it can be active rhythmically the more it remains alive in its inmost nature. Where it is deprived of rhythm and can no longer flow freely in meanders, or trickle over stones and murmur and chatter and form waves, it begins gradually to grow weary and die. Then it loses its ability to mediate between heaven and earth.

In the living kingdoms of nature water is the bearer of the rhythmical processes—in the rise and fall of the sap in plants and in the pulsation of the bodily fluids in man and animal. Here too, it maintains within itself the manifold rhythms of the earth-organism and the universe, passing them on to the beings of the earth.

It is in the nature of water that it possesses those characteristics fundamental to all organisms for the maintenance of their life; yet all is purely functional and without fixed form. These living qualities are nevertheless so clearly present and so evidently at work, that the picture of the human organism is conjured up before us in its three-fold nature—metabolic, nerve-sense and rhythmic organisations—revealing in harmony the basic characteristics of all living organisms. What in water is still entirely intermingled and united, is in man and animal specialised out into three processes, appearing as particular organic functions and even solidified and condensed into the respective organic forms. In the following chapters we shall study three such organs: the ear, a sense organ; the intestine, an organ of metabolism; and the heart as the centre of the rhythmical organisation of man. They remind us of the three characteristics of water; or vice versa, water can remind us of the three organic systems of the human being.

The Ear

The sense organ with which we can perceive something of the inner nature of things, the ear, itself retreats from our observation deep into an interior space of its own. An extremely delicate structure, it lies, surrounded and filled with fluid, in a cave of the hardest "rock", like the spiral shell of a snail, which has secreted hard substance around itself as a protection. Together with the neighbouring semi-circular canals, this organ is one of the most sensitive in our whole organism. A glance at the external ear sees the spiral form winding its way into the internal ear and becoming lost there. Like a vortex with its funnel, the ear conch and the ear passage lead to the first membrane, the ear-drum, against which the ossicles of the middle ear lean. Like a minute "system of limbs" (R. Steiner), they pass on the rhythms they receive to the membrane of the fenestra ovalis in the internal ear, where they are led still deeper into the dark regions of the cochlea. The passage into the cavity of the internal ear is like a journey through the elements, from air via the solid medium to the liquid, and every form on the way reveals its origin in the arche-typal movements of fluids.

This can be seen especially in the organ closely related to the coch-lea—the semicircular canals. These also develop out of the first vesicle of the ear. In three small curved canals, set vertically to one another, there is a liquid, and every movement of the head causes this liquid to move within the walls of the canals. Sensory hair cells protruding into the liquid take up the stimulus of the movement and inform us as to our movement and position in space. The organ is based on revolving movements of liquid in a closed circulation. Some lower animals, for instance the river-lamprey, have only one of these canals; instead of the other two they have cavities in which a liquid, actively agitated by cilia, is driven round in tiny vortices. The semicircular canal that appears at a later stage in the development of animals is here still only in the realm of function and movement, thus revealing the basic principle of formation. A structure intersecting itself three times, and as though emerging out of vortical movement, is built into man, giving him the capacity to hold himself erect, to move and to experience himself in space. In the semicircular canals we have an image of the surface returning into itself with which projective geometry deals, (pictured in Boy's model of the plane at infinity).

Geometrical form after Boy's model of the plane at infinity

The membranous cochlea of the internal ear, a tube filled and surrounded with fluid and having a blind extremity, combines the spiralling surface—an archetypal form of flowing movement—with the spiral twisting of a vortex. The vortex, which otherwise appears in a liquid, is here moulded into a perfect, most delicately differentiated sense organ. The formative principle of the curling, rolled in

The cochlea of the human ear (after de Burlet); the semi-circular canals are omitted

In the cochlea, the basilar membrane spirals up to the apex, getting wider towards the top

An object moved backwards and forwards in water creates a field of vortices

surface of contact between different regions of liquid permeates the whole ear. It is as though in the embryonic development of the human ear the sacculus were drawn with a force of mighty suction into a liquid vortex, its surface rolled up to form the sensitive boundary membrane and at the same time twisted through 90 degrees.

Thus in the internal ear the two scalae are like the two regions of liquid, on either side of a boundary layer; they hold the really sensitive organ between them and develop it further. It must be realised that in the phylogenetic development of the organ of hearing there is no actual occurrence of circulating liquids—apart from what we have already described regarding the vortex cavities in the labyrinth of the river-lamprey. It is rather as though the rotating principle as a force were invisibly to permeate and guide the embryonic intucking. A time-lapse photograph of the development of the cochlea would certainly reveal a movement like that of a vortex in a liquid. Vortices with a distinct spiral twist may also arise when rhythmical impulses influence a fluid at rest, for instance the movement to and fro of an object on the surface of water. A system of adjacent vortices—for example, four lying side by side—results from movements of this kind.

Taking into account that in the process of hearing, incessant rhythmical impulses are inflicted from without upon the fenestra ovalis—a delicate membrane leading to the fluid in the internal ear —one can understand how this vortex-like organ might develop out of the world of rhythmical sounds; it is formed by sound for sound. (An appropriate alteration of Goethe's words.) Indeed, the lengthening and curling in of the ductus endolymphaticus, filled with fluid, is not found in the development of animals until they leave the element of water and step on to dry land; the rhythmical sounds in the atmosphere begin to vibrate into their watery world. In crocodiles and birds the cochlea formation begins to develop in the ear. One might think of writing the names of the different species on the different parts of the cochlea, indicating how far each had come in the spiral development of the organ. Here again a corresponding time-lapse photograph could show a vortex movement in the gradual development of the ears of the animals. However, the animal nature sometimes overshoots the mark, creating a record number of twists in the spiral, though they thus forfeit the harmonious moderation found in the cochlea of the human being; for instance in the agouti, a rodent, the cochlea has five twists. This does, however, reveal the spiral structure of the cochlea all the more clearly.

Furthermore, in the actual process of hearing, the vortex that has found a solid shape in the internal ear is permeated by the circulating, whirling movements of liquid. A boundary surface separating the scalae, the basilar membrane creates a characteristic train of waves for each note, imparting it to the neighbouring fluid above and below, which curls in to form vortices, just as in the case of the boundary surface between two flowing streams. Only the principle is reversed; here the dividing surface itself provides the movement of the travelling waves, causing vortex formations in the neighbouring otherwise quiescent liquid. Each note has its own consistent spot on the sensitive membrane, where for it the wave and vortex formations are most clearly marked. High notes are localised at the lower end, near the fenestra ovalis, and low notes at the upper end near the apex of the cochlea.

As the sounds of the external world enter, whole vortex trains pass through the fluid of the internal ear. In connection with this a sorting out of rhythms takes place, by which the long wave trains of the low frequency low notes reach the end of the basilar membrane, while the short, quick rhythms of the high notes fade away right at the start. On a minute scale and as an organic function, this is the counterpart to the great sorting out process of the different types of waves in the oceans of the earth. (See the chapter: The Wave.) In the ocean, too, the different wave lengths are sorted out; the larger ones overtake the smaller ones and after long journeys reach distant coasts, while the smaller waves have "echoed away" after a short distance. The sorting out that takes place in the internal ear can thus be compared to an analysis, a splitting up into the constituent components, followed, however, by a synthesis, in which the human being reassembles what has been separated, piecing the sound image together again into a body of sound. This process is analogous to that of metabolism, where all nourishment is at first broken down before being built up again and integrated into the organism in a composition fitting to the nature of each human being. This is a creative activity in the realm of number ratios, on the one hand in the realm of sound or music, on the other in the process of breaking down and building up of substances, where whole-number proportions prevail. Processes of hearing echo on in the processes of metabolism. In analogy with the metabolism of substances, one might call the process of hearing a metabolism of sound, in which the

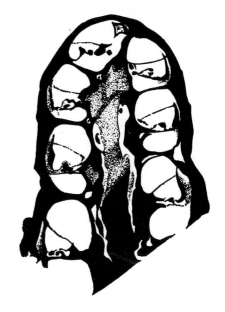

Cross-section of the cochlea of a guinea-pig (from De Burlet)

The form of vibration of the basilar membrane. For simplification the spiral of the cochlea has been drawn out straight (after v. Békésy)

Distribution of sensitivity to tones in the cochlea: high notes are localised near the stapes, and low notes near the apex of the cochlea

sounds taken in are broken down and then built up again according to the musical number ratios inherent in them.

Thus it is as though the rhythmical play of the fluid element in waves and vortices at the sensitive boundary surfaces, and the interpenetration of rhythms is met with again in a concentrated form—condensed into an actual sense-organ—in the processes of the internal ear. Withdrawn from observation, they reveal the inner nature of those processes expressed in the experience of sound, welling up in the soul life of the human being. In man, the processes we have been describing find their equivalent at a higher and more real level of existence. Indeed, man even builds his body with the help of these processes, for it is permeated through and through with musical rhythms and numerical proportions. Greatest of the secrets hidden in flowing liquids is that the harmony of the spheres resounds and vibrates within them. In the ear they have become sense organ! The phenomena in flowing liquids provide a key for man; he may see reflected in them the splendour of the harmonies of the spheres.

The Intestine

In the organ of hearing the three principles—spiralling surface, sensitive membrane and rhythmical activity—unite in the field of sensitivity and create a most delicate organ, finely formed and chiselled in every detail. We find these same principles again, of course, in the intestine. Now, however, according to the intestine's own function they are to a great extent withdrawn from the sphere of form and manifest in the plasticity of rhythmical movement. Accordingly, the capacity to perceive consciously is lost in the dark realm of metabolic activity. The whole formation of the intestines is directed towards the breaking down, liquefaction, destruction, permeation and transport of substances. And as in the process the substance becomes liquid, it may be supposed from the start that the

The digestive tract is rhythmically articulated in expansion and contraction (diagram after Rauber-Kopsch)

paths along which it wanders will correspond to the archetypal movements of the liquid element. Just as we see naturally flowing water moving in meanders, curves and spiralling loops, rhythmically creating its own river bed, so now we recognise these processes in digestion.

The spiralling surface is the guiding principle, but the forms are not greatly differentiated; rather is the formative force to some extent withdrawn in favour of movement and the destroying of form.

The digestive tract as a whole, starting at the lips, is not simply a cylindrical pipe, but a rhythmically articulated structure dividing the process of metabolism in space and time into several main parts, in expansion and contraction. It is as though this rhythm has become a form and superimposed on it is the peristalsis of the intestine which is still purely movement.

The inner ear does not enter into any material relationship with what it perceives; it is connected with the object of its perception through the element of rhythmical movement inherent in its form and substance. The opposite is the case with the intestine. Substance fills out the organ, is broken down and disintegrated within it and at the same time set in most intensive and varied motion. Substance surrenders itself entirely in the intestinal process. In the realm of sound the material world merely communicates its inmost being in sounds or tones.

The varied movements of the liquid substance along the intestine in curving surfaces, meanders and spiralling streams can be studied in the animal world in great variety. A few illustrations will serve here.

The drawing on page 24 shows the intestine of the lung-fish; a fully formed spiral fold imprints a corresponding movement on to the substance within it. Cryptoplax oculatus manifests this movement by twisting the intestine itself into screw-like formations. The large intestine of some animals, for instance the rabbit, shows a distinctly formed spiral which reappears in the appendix as a counter spiral. In the pig, the large intestine in particular is formed in several spiralling twists. Cattle, fundamentally creatures of digestion, have in their intestines a curling and uncurling spiral much like that of the ear.

What in the human being appears only as the indication of a spiralling fold at the very end of the intestine, is found in cattle as the shape of the organ as a *whole*; the liquid, plastic stream of nourishing

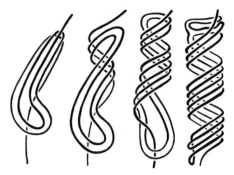

Development of the intestine of cryptoplax oculatus (from Ludwig)

Intestine and appendix of the rabbit (after Zietschmann)

Intestinal convolutions of the pig (after Zietschmann)

89

The spiral convolutions in the intestines of cattle are formed to perfection (after Zietschmann)

substance wanders through the intestine according to the typical movement of flowing liquid. This formation in man is more restrained; he does not become a creature of digestion, but reserves his forces for spiritual activity.

Calling to mind that the movements of a fluid vortex imitate a planetary system in miniature, and seeing that a similar movement is imprinted upon the nutritive liquid, for instance in the intestines of cattle, we have a picture of substance being led from a planetary periphery to a sunlike centre and then spread out again into a periphery, while at the same time it is being thoroughly broken down and transmuted. It is a process which, if we consider the numerical relationships to be found in its rhythms, is akin to the world of sound.[1]

Diagram of the heart, early stage in fish, (after Nierstrasz)

The Heart

In the ear and in the intestine we have polarities, inasmuch as the organ of hearing belongs to the nerve-sense organisation and the organ of digestion to the metabolic processes that take place in the unconscious. The heart lies spatially and also functionally between the two. It is as though the two "streams", one from above, the other from below, meet in the heart and are balanced there in a primal rhythm.

Even a simple diagram of the heart reveals the movement on which it is based. The pattern resembles that made when a stream of liquid flows into still water, or when streams of liquid meet under water, where a rhythmical series of regions in the water are separated off, alternately accepting and rejecting space (Plate 47). The whole func-

The heart of the cockchafer, a rhythmical sequence of chambers (after Schmeil)

[1] In spiritual science we learn of the activity of the chemical- or sound-ether in connection with number ratios in the realm of sound and in chemical processes. The chemical-ether permeates in particular the world of the watery element, and, as bearer of sound, the region of the air also.

tion and form of the heart is a reflection of the streaming processes of water, where in its movements of expansion and contraction it is as though separate spaces were continually being formed. The hearts of some lower animals show a cavity formation similar to that in water. A long series of identical chambers are formed, in which the blood has to contract and expand as it flows through. In these hearts a wall surrounds what in the water is simply a pulsating stream; it serves to make the process more clearly visible. The organ pulsates in the rhythm of the stream of liquid out of which it has been shaped, thus simply making this rhythm visible.

In an experiment, two elastic vessels may be placed in water and caused to pulsate uniformly, like the chambers of the heart; currents will arise between them. If solid particles are added to the water they arrange themselves around the vessels in ridges vertical to the current. The ridges lie round the pulsating chambers in Cassini ovals like the corresponding muscle fibres around the pulsating heart chambers. It must not be forgotten that the very pulsating motion itself belongs to the nature of flowing liquid. Taking our start from facts like these, there is no need to imagine the activity of the heart to be that of a pump.

In the human heart, form and movement are interrelated, uniting in a rhythmical process in space and time. The organ, a form in space, is at the same time a movement in time.

This organ is like a vortical centre of suction to which the blood rushes with ever increasing speed from the periphery, thence to return again, slowing down and spreading out. It is an image of a planetary system with a sunlike centre of infinite dynamic force. The speed in the centre of a vortex tends to become inconceivably great; but infinite speeds are not possible on earth, hence the suction.

A vortex often pulsates in itself. Keeping a strict rhythm, it widens, growing shorter, and then contracts, growing longer. In the heart, the archetypal movements, superimposed on one another, result in the formation of the separate chambers; these rhythms merge and interpenetrate in the pulsating vortex.

The fibres of the heart are a physical echo of the creative movements by which it was begotten. In spiralling paths they swing down to its apex and then rise again to its base. They make the same movements and emphasise the revolving vortical streaming of the fluids within the heart.

In the lung-fish a spiral fold is even built into the centre of the blood stream, dividing the lumen into two halves, in which the two kinds

Solid particles are deposited in curves of Cassini in the field of currents arising around two uniformly pulsating chambers

Fibres in the left chamber of the human heart (after Benninghoff)

of blood flow separately. An observer thinking only of utility will see in this merely a division between the two kinds of blood. But if we think of the inner dynamic quality of the process itself we see that even without such a fold the blood stream will remain divided into two parts, contiguous in a surface. It is as though this surface were to suck the living material to itself and appear as a visible fold. According to how an elastic pipe is bent, the surface of contact between the two secondary streams is twisted within the pipe (see page 22).

Spiralling fibres at the apex of the heart (after Benninghoff)

The heart, then, a rhythmical organ, is formed from the intertwining, spiralling fibres and surfaces, which consolidate out of the pulsating, flowing movement. In this process the movement is not altered; rather do the surfaces grow into what has already been invisibly pre-formed.

Besides the rhythmical activity we may also expect to find the quality of sensitivity in the blood stream of the heart. An examination of the formation of the nervous system of the heart will show, that even in simply constructed hearts the sensitive places are to be found just at those points where in a stream of liquid we would expect to find sensitive places. These places occur wherever the stream contracts and has to pass through a narrow space, creating as it does a moving layer of surfaces.[1] Here too it is as though an organ, at first concealed in the flowing stream of blood, becomes consolidated into a finished form. Various receptive centres, points sensitive to the different qualities of the blood stream and its composition, may be found in the heart. It is permeated through and through with a delicate capacity of perception through which it takes account of the messages brought to it from the organism by the blood. It is like the sun centre of the organism itself, which "hears and speaks" in order to co-ordinate the whole organism with its inner reciprocal relationships into the living rhythms of time. No wonder it is connected via the rhythm of breathing with the rhythms of the cosmic sun year, which for its part co-ordinates the systems of planetary movement to form an organism.

The centres of automatic action in the heart of a fish are situated at the "sensitive" points in the stream, where it narrows (from Buddenbrock, after v. Skramlik)

It is not our purpose here to consider in all detail the anatomical structure and physiology of various organs. We are concerned to indicate a direction towards the understanding of the creation of organic forms. In considering these three organs we have attempted to point the way to such an understanding, and above all to show how in flowing water the archetypal images of the threefold nature of man with all his organs are contained. Accordingly the blood, itself a liquid and therefore still unformed, bears these archetypal images within it and materialises them anew at every moment, out of its streaming movement. The blood is indeed the *archetypal organ of liquid flow*. As a liquid it has all organic formation potentially within it. As "blood" it is the expression of the spiritual being according to the Idea of whom the various organs are moulded and assembled to form a total organism—the body in which this being may live.

If therefore blood is an expression of the being ruling over it, may we not ask if there is a similar higher being of whom water, the "blood of the earth", is the physical expression?

---

[1] We shall show later how defiles like this are always places of heightened sensitivity.

Streaming Wisdom

We have now come so far in our considerations that we must take into account a possible objection, namely, that the organs of the human being and of animals and all plant forms do indeed arise out of the watery element, but their development takes place in an altogether different measure of time. The organic forms created by flowing water appear for a moment, only to recede again and become invisible. The forms of living organs seem to have arisen out of flowing movements, and to manifest the laws of water, but they take a long time to become actual visible forms in material substance. In organic formation there are no currents flowing with the speed of a stream, and all processes are completed with hardly any apparent movement. In water, forms appear and disappear in a moment; in the organs they are gradually created and transformed. It is as though there were a world of forces creating and fashioning the organs, and certainly working according to the laws of water, but in the invisible; there is a world of forces which mould a form again and again in streaming repetition, while material substance becomes gradually assimilated into it. The organic form slowly and gently appears, as though surrounded and permeated by invisible streams. Observation of the development of living creatures points to such a world of forces. This world is concealed from direct sense observation, but we may perceive its signature, inscribed in and with water as though by an invisible hand. The spiritual science of Rudolf Steiner describes this invisible and therefore supersensible world of forces and calls them etheric formative forces, the forces imbued with life in the etheric bodies of living creatures.

The etheric body of the human being is the body of forces, hidden from the senses, on which the physical body is founded. It permeates the physical body at every moment and saves it from solid rigidity and death. If the etheric body leaves the physical body, the latter is immediately given over to the forces of disintegration of the dead mineral world and becomes once more a part of this world. Thus the etheric body is constantly engaged in a struggle with the purely earthly laws; it is described as that aspect of the living body which confronts weight with lightness or upthrust; it meets the physical forces of pressure with those of suction. It is the bearer of the universal forces of the cosmos, the counterpart of the centric forces of the earth.

The etheric body takes part in the gradual changes in the heavenly processes, which hold sway in everlasting movement, creation and transformation of form in the eternal stream of time. The cosmic qualities and movements of water, which we have attempted to describe above, are images of the etheric stream and as such they are also its mediators in the material world. All the qualities of water are akin to this world of etheric forces, and constantly express it. The laws of the etheric world are mirrored in the world of water and they carry on a constant creative dialogue. So we can understand from another angle how the element of water can also be an element of the cosmos, of the waters of the heavens, in which the "boats of the star gods" weave their forms and shapes as though in a heavenly script.

All organic formation is based on this world of etheric forces, which in turn receives formative impulses from the spiritual world. The etheric forces use the appropriate medium of water, which vibrates in resonance with them, thus passing on the formative impulses to the material world.

Withdrawn from our waking consciousness, these forces are active when our body is being formed within the maternal organism; indeed they stream around our organs as long as we are alive. Part of them can be released once the organs have been formed and only need to be maintained. It is one of the great discoveries made by Rudolf Steiner that the forces needed for the creation of the organs are gradually freed during childhood and can then be seen to be at work in the conscious life of the human being. They appear as the forces which help the child to stand upright, to walk, to speak and finally to think.

In these activities of man, arising through the power of the etheric forces, we should be able to find the traces of the etheric forces, in which they are still entirely steeped, indeed of which they are to a great extent the expression. We shall discuss the realm of the forces of speech later; for the moment we will turn briefly to the connection of thinking with the etheric world.

The bodily instrument of thinking, the brain, in its spherical form, mirrors the planetary and cosmic laws. It rests in the "waters of the world" and is to a great extent withdrawn from the earthly laws of gravity through the force of buoyancy. Its undulations are the movements of the etheric element of "water" which have become *organ*; they have been laid down in flowing lines. We have here, in a play of repetition, the basic theme of the meander. Is it surprising if this formative force, once it has been freed from actually forming the organ, should reappear in the flow of thought? Does not this etheric force, for ever multiplying, reappear in the ability of thinking to be able always to repeat what has once been thought? Constant repetition is characteristic of water and of the etheric, so also of thinking. Inherent in memory is the capacity of being able to rethink any number of times what has been thought before.

In the world of living creatures this principle of repetition appears in great variety, e.g. in the formation of segments, vertebrae, metameric organs, for instance in the primitive kidney, and in many other examples. Reproduction, repetition in propagation, appears in the organic world as well as in the flowing of water and in the spiritual life of the human being. When learning something by heart, the more often we repeat it rhythmically, again and again, the better it impresses itself upon us and becomes a permanent memory and ability. But also it is all the easier to understand something the more it is examined, felt and grasped from all sides. This spiritual activity too has its expression in the liquid element, which envelops objects from all sides, grasps and feels and goes thoroughly into every detail of a form.

The activity of thinking is essentially an expression of flowing movement. Only when thinking dwells on a particular content, a particular form, does it order itself accordingly and create an idea. Every idea—like every organic form—arises in a process of flow, until the movement congeals into a form. Therefore we speak of a capacity to think fluently when someone is skilfully able to carry out this creation of form in thought, harmoniously co-ordinating the stream of thoughts and progressing from one idea to another without digression—without creating "whirlpools". We say of someone who is less successful in this that his thinking is languid and sluggish. An exercise suggested by Rudolf Steiner to help thinking to become fluent and mobile is to recreate and transform in thought, for instance, cloud formations. With this ability to enter thoughtfully into everything and to picture all things in the form of ideas, the process of thinking partakes in the laws of the formative processes of the universe. These are the same laws as at work in the fluid element, which renounces a form of its own and is prepared to enter into all things, to unite all things, to absorb all things.

Thinking that cannot enter deeply enough into every detail becomes a flight of ideas, torn along as though by an invisible torrent in which it can create no permanent forms. On the other hand, thinking that becomes solidified in fixed ideas remains a captive of form, without being able to develop towards further possibilities. Like water, thought can create forms, can unite and relate the forms to one another as ideas; it can unite, but also separate and analyse. The capacity of water in the realm of substance to dissolve and bind together reappears in thinking as a spiritual activity.

Water and this spiritual activity of the human being belong together; the nature of the one is a picture of the other. Both can unite with the earth, while at the same time receiving the ideas of the universe, uniting and co-ordinating them. In thinking there prevails the etheric life of the water forces; through water flows the wisdom of the universe. Is it not this wisdom itself which has created the element of water, a tool for its own activity?

7—DSC

On the Spiritual Nature of the Liquid Element

"It is really vain to attempt to express the nature of something. We notice effects, and a complete account of these effects would perhaps comprise the nature of this thing. We attempt in vain to describe the character of a man; but a description of his actions and his deeds will create for us a picture of his character" (Goethe: *Theory of Colour*).

Let us examine water with this in mind.

Wherever there is water, life can become active in the material world; where there is no water this possibility ceases. Water is essentially the element of life, wherever possible it wrests life from death. It is the great healer of all that is sick and has lost its living poise; for water forever strives after balance, a living balance, never a static one that would extinguish life. It is everywhere a mediator between contrasts, which grow sharper where it is absent. Thus it brings together elements hostile to one another, constantly creating something new out of them. It dissolves what is solid, rendering it back to life.

In itself water remains chemically neutral, but it does unite with other substances where the solid element is too much in opposition to life. Water desires nothing for itself, it gives of itself freely, never questioning the form into which it must change when needed by a plant, an animal or man; with the same submissiveness it fills them all. It resigns itself selflessly to every need, retiring after acting as mediator, to be ready for new creativity. As in its very nature it is itself pure, it can purify, refresh, heal, strengthen, revive and clarify all things. "Water is the element of selfless contrast, it passively exists for others . . . water's existence is thus an existing-for-others. . . . It is its fate to be something not yet specialised . . . and therefore it soon came to be called 'the mother of all that is special' " (Hegel, *Naturphilosophie II. Teil*).

Water does not close itself to light as does a solid body, but makes itself clear and transparent; in the pure play of colour in the rainbow it attains the fullness of possibilities. Selflessly it is mediator, in the eye for the impressions of the visible world, in the ear for those of the audible world. But it also opens itself to the harmonies and laws of the heavens, which it passes on to the growing human embryo, surrounding it entirely. It also passes these laws on to the thoughtful human being via a watery sphere with which it surrounds his organ of thinking. To a great extent withdrawn from the force of gravity, it maintains a central position between earth and cosmos, never losing itself to the one or the other and yet remaining closely connected with both, uniting them in an eternal circulation. Water holds a balance between extremes of solidification and evaporation, always retaining its possibilities of transformation. Like an echo of the ever changing events of the heavens, the fullness of form in the world comes forth from water.

Not only does water give to the human being and to all living nature the basis for existence in a living body, but it pictures—as though in a great parable—higher qualities of man's development. Qualities such as the overcoming of rigidity in thought, of prejudice, of intolerance; the ability to enter into all things and to learn to understand them out of their own nature and to create out of polarities a higher unity; all these are aims of human striving which we can recognise also in the qualities of water. They represent ways in which man may win through to selflessness in a pure, healthy and light-filled soul life. Just as water aids him in his entry into the earthly world, mediating to him the heavenly forces, so it can also lead him to a rebirth of his spiritual nature. Touching upon these possibilities of development, Wolfram von Eschenbach speaks of the nature of water:

"... He also went into the water for baptism from Whom Adam received his features. From water, trees derive their sap. Water fructifies all created things, which man calls creatures. From water man has his sight. Water gives many souls such radiance that angels cannot be more bright."

Parcival XVI, 817.

Translated by H. M. Mustard and C. E. Passage.

Water and Air

In the preceding pages, water has been discussed as the representative of all that is liquid, but the fact has not yet been taken into account that water is always permeated with air or other gases, which are dissolved in it. This means that in all the processes that have hitherto been described, the gaseous condition plays a certain, though minor, part, and that the laws of the element of air play into the element of water and vice versa (Plates 79 and 80). Wherever water flows, foaming and bubbling, or where it cascades and tumbles over stones, air is taken in and unites with it. The colder the water is, the more gases it can absorb, among which oxygen and carbon dioxide play an essential part.

Oxygen is of great importance for the natural purification of water and for all life within it. *How* important the intake of oxygen is, may be seen where this gas is absent in water, as a result of which the life in it is extinguished. This happens when water no longer moves sufficiently to allow it to be thoroughly permeated with air (stagnant water), or when the bed of the water is covered with so much rotting sludge, for instance through waste drainage, that the oxygen content of the water is no longer sufficient to break it down.

Cold water can absorb more oxygen than warm, which may have been the reason why in olden days fields were successfully irrigated in winter instead of in summer.

The respiration of water animals is adjusted entirely according to the air and oxygen content of the water; they cannot live if there is too little oxygen dissolved in it. It is as though their gills were consolidations of the great inner surfaces of the streaming water itself; these surfaces we have seen to be related to processes of life. Here they serve to bring the oxygen in the water into the inner life processes of the creatures living in it.

The organic world of plants in lakes and seas is dependent on the content of carbon dioxide in the water. It is a process of cosmic proportions when in the changing seasons, with their growth and decline of vegetation, the carbon dioxide is inhaled and exhaled by the water of the oceans. If the carbon dioxide content of the air increases, the water immediately begins to absorb the surplus; if it decreases, the water releases it again, until a balance is achieved between the content of carbon dioxide in the water and that in the atmosphere. Thus when in autumn the plant world withers away and no longer inhales carbon dioxide, and in the breaking down processes of plant substance, in the disintegrating foliage, much carbon dioxide is released into the air, this is absorbed by the seas. When, however, in spring the plant world grows anew and forms the substance for its foliage out of the carbon dioxide in the air, the waters of the earth once again release some of the necessary carbon dioxide. Through this carbon dioxide cycle the whole building up and breaking down process of the plant world is integrated into the earth's great system of respiration.

This property of water to form reservoirs of carbon dioxide is yet another of the ways in which it promotes life on the earth. We have seen how the seas are the great reservoirs of warmth on this planet and how they regulate the climate; we now find that they are also the great regulators of the respiratory processes over the whole earth. Indeed, in its ability to absorb gases, water is mediator for the whole metabolism of the oceans on a grand scale. By absorbing carbon dioxide it increases its ability to dissolve solid substances. Water containing a large amount of carbon dioxide can, for instance, absorb more limestone than water containing only a little. Accompanying the play between the absorption out of the air and the release into the air of carbon dioxide, is a simultaneous "metabolism" of the limestone content of the water.

This metabolism within the oceans is of great significance for the development of life in them. And so, with its ability to absorb gases, water brings together the life on the solid continents with that in the deep seas; both regions depend on one another and form a unity. The life of each single creature can only be understood in relation to the life of the whole planet, in which—a small part of a great whole—it is embedded.

The laws of air and gas play their part in the inner life processes of organisms. Diffusion and osmosis are an expression of these laws; even quantitively they are subject to them. But it is water which makes it possible for these processes to take place, thus rendering yet another service to life. This does not mean to say that the nature of the life processes is solely that of diffusion and osmosis: indeed, in many cases these are overcome by the processes of life.

As water on the one hand absorbs gases, so on the other it is prepared to relinquish its liquid form for a time and become vaporous. There is in the lower layers of the earth's atmosphere no air which does not contain water. Indeed, the water contained in the air is the incentive for all meteorological events in the atmospheric mantle of the earth. Nearly all the different kinds of precipitation consist of water which has previously evaporated into the air. As it comes into contact with the air it dissolves into it until the saturation point of the air is reached. Every waterfall dissolves at its edges into an infinite number of the tiniest droplets, forming an inconceivable extent of surface at which the two elements meet and there the water surrenders itself to the air. The opposite process may be observed wherever water cascades and pours over stones into a pool. Air is then swept into the water, sparkling in white bubbles and creating great surfaces of contact at which the water can "breathe" (Plates 2 and 4). So air takes part in the streaming movements of water, just as, in the play of clouds, water vapours join in the movements of the air (Plate 80).

Thus air and water mingle in an intermediate region; they move mainly according to the laws of liquid flow. Air complies to a great extent with these laws, only fully asserting its own nature under certain circumstances. We may therefore expect to find in air many of the forms of movement familiar to us in water, though often on a larger scale or at greater speeds.

In a stream, where water flows over stones, waves are formed, through which new water constantly flows. The same happens when air flows over a mountain range; behind the mountains just such waves arise, with new air constantly flowing through them. The waves are of course invisible in the transparent air, but sometimes in the high crests of the waves the water contained in the air separates out in the form of clouds, thus making the crests visible as elongated, fish-shaped clouds, lying one behind the other. Between the separate clouds we may imagine the trough of the wave in which, because it lies lower, the water vapour does not appear as a cloud (Plate 77). These waves sometimes remain in one place for hours on end, though new air is constantly streaming through them; they remain until the stream of air comes to rest or changes its direction. The wisp of cloud clinging to the peak of the Matterhorn is an example of a similar process; though it remains constant as a form, its substance changes moment by moment.

Spiralling and screw-like surfaces, too, appear in air as well as in water. We all know the spiralling formations made in the air by rising steam or smoke. Smoke and steam show how air goes through all the elements of movement that we have been examining in water. All the kinds of movement we have been studying, from the simple wave formation to the complicated formations of spiralling and in-curling surfaces, we find again here. What is **so** difficult to observe in water can be seen in the air over every cup of tea or burning cigarette.

Horizontal layers of revolving air over the desert. Gliding birds make use of the ascending currents (after Idrac)

Idrac observed these movements in air on a large scale over the wide, hot spaces of the Sahara. Enormous cylinders of air with horizontal axes are made visible through the flight of desert birds. These birds glide in their thousands in long lines reaching from one horizon to the other. They hover on the ascending air currents between two adjacent cylinders or rollers of moving air.

Vertical cylinders of air may also be found towering over the land. Gliding birds make use of their upward stream and are often carried to great heights.

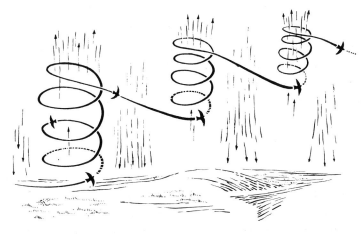

Vertically spiralling columns of air. Gliding birds are carried by them to great heights (after Idrac)

Vortices and trains of vortices arise in air, as in water, when it has to stream round obstacles. Wind forms vortices wherever it is obstructed by trees or branches, roofs or chimney-stacks. But because of the greater speed of air these will follow very much faster on one another than they would in the same process in water. In these high speeds, air begins to show something of its own nature, for now the rapidly forming sequence of vortices becomes audible. The gale howls around roofs and chimney-pots and whistles through the woods. Every pine needle and every tiny twig causes trains of vortices to arise; the vortices follow so closely on one another that the whistling, rushing sound arises. A wood of conifers breaks up the streaming air into an unbelievable number of tiny vortices. Here, too, there arise those vast extents of surface which in water we saw to be like sensitive "organs". The moving forms are the same, but because of the greater speeds the air begins to differ from the element of water. What in air is audible, is silent in water. What is a sounding process in air, is slowed down in water and becomes visible as form.

Water in the Atmospheric Mantle of the Earth

Everywhere in nature the elements of air and water mingle in manifold interplay. Every system of rivers, every lake, every sea, is an organic totality with its own circulation, and to each of these belongs the air space above it. Every river, lake, or sea-coast makes itself felt in the air above it, up to a great height. On misty days a pilot can often see the courses of the rivers as banks of mist below him; but also on days without mist he can tell by the behaviour of his machine when he is flying over a river or lake, or whether he is over a wood or an open stretch of field, for their borders have an effect in the air above.

The air space above a piece of land forms with it a whole, and the air moves accordingly. In summer, air descends over the cool lakes and woods, and ascends over the warmer fields. If there is considerable cooling at night it can happen that the open country becomes cooler than the surrounding woods or stretches of water, so that the movements of air are reversed in a rhythm of day and night. The air is always ascending over the warmer land and descending over the cooler. Circulations arising in the air spaces over a tract of land express something of its life and belong to it entirely.

Air currents over woodland and open field

There are circulations like this in the whole atmosphere of the earth. What takes place on a small scale over woods and lakes occurs on a large scale over the seas; and what takes place over fields and meadows is repeated over the continents. In winter the relationship is reversed on the small as well as on the large scale, because in winter water is warmer than the dry land.

These ascending and descending movements of air form the great areas of the earth into a vast organism. The rhythm of day and night in the circulation of the small land areas has its equivalent in the rhythms of the seasons of summer and winter over the whole planet. In the warm season of the year, the air rises over the continents and falls over the seas; in the cold season this movement is reversed. An ascending movement of air is among other things connected with the formation of regions of low pressure, and descending air with regions of high pressure. In this way, towards summer, a great region of low pressure spreads out over the Central Asian continent, which towards winter becomes transformed into a region of high pressure centred over Asia. These processes are an integral part of the great seasonal breathing of the earth, as described by Wachsmuth.

In connection with the movements of air we have just described, there is also an expansion and contraction according to heat or cold which occurs in the rhythms of the seasons. The meteorologists speak of the "breathing of the continents". In the transition periods between summer and winter, in other words, in spring and autumn, the transformation or changeover of the so-called stationary regions of high and low pressure takes place; summer and winter meet in rhythmical combat.

The regions of high and low pressure are by no means simply regions in which air ascends or descends. The air masses of these regions are caused to follow a spiralling course by the revolutions of the earth, whereby the spiral movement of the vortex appears even on this enormous scale. The spiralling formation, which so often accompanies movement of any kind, also appears here.

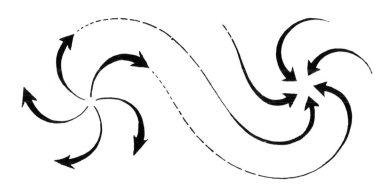

Regions of high and low pressure.
High: descending winds spreading out over the ground
Low: winds converging over the ground and then ascending

If we were to imagine ourselves situated high above the surface of the earth and presume that we were able to perceive the air currents in the summer as they ascend over the continents and descend over the oceans, we should be presented with an extremely varied picture. Embedded in the spacious movements of the atmospheric mantle of the earth we should see, like many "organs", the smaller circulatory systems of air over the different parts of the land, over woodland, field, lake, river, mountain or valley. We should see the picture of a great organism in which the smaller "organs" are embedded, every one connected with all the others, all connected together through a lively interplay of movements and currents in the air.

We have already met with the picture of an organism like this in water, in the interplay between sources and sinks, where forms of an organic nature are created. In the air the ascending and descending currents, as seen from a height, correspond to these sources and sinks. They translate the movement of the landscape below them into an interplay of ascending and descending movements in the air. In this way earth, air and water are united in one great whole in which each preserves its own nature and yet moves together with the others, becoming alive in the great and small rhythms of summer and winter, day and night. Indeed, each movement in the air during the course of a day has a rhythm of its own; all the many ascending and descending movements take place not uniformly but in rhythmically repeated thrusts. It is as though, in separate delicate breaths, the landscape were to "speak" into the air around it.

The question remains as to where in the organism of landscape and earth the surfaces are to be found which in water, in the interplay between sources and sinks, are of such significance. For it is along these surfaces that the rhythmical movements of waves and vortices pass. Surfaces like these may indeed also be found in the air.

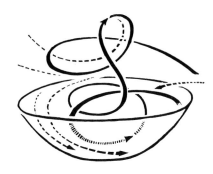

Wind in an area of low pressure (after Blanc)

High   Low

Regions of high and low pressure in January

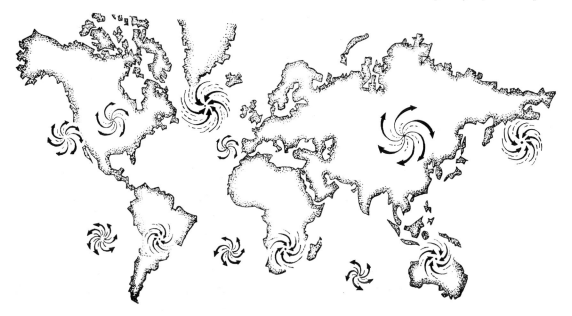

Wherever in a landscape these ascending and descending currents meet, such invisible surfaces arise. A glider pilot can often recognise them in passing, like delicately turbulent "curtains" that hang, as it were, in the air. They occur, for example, where the landscape below him changes from woodland to open field. They are simply the spiralled surfaces of contact between different masses of air.

In the great spaces of air around the earth similar dividing surfaces arise at the "fronts", the frontiers between different kinds of air, namely, wherever the regions of influence of the great sources and sinks, the stationary regions of high and low pressure, meet. The same forms which we found when examining water may be found again in the great currents of air around the earth. Everywhere at the surfaces of the great cloud masses we may find the play of waves, invaginations and curling movements, which we observed to be the archetypal movements in the formation of organs. We look here into a world of creative processes, in which everything remains in movement, in which organs are laid down but never become solidified, always being led back again to movement.[1]

High cloud mass shaped like a living organ,
over Europe on 6th March, 1943
(after Kleinschmidt)

Processes quite similar to the dropping in of masses of cold air from the poles into the warmer air masses of the lower latitudes may be found in the development of the neural tube or the eye in the human embryo.

[1] Considerations with regard to unstable surfaces in the atmosphere in connection with atomic explosions appear in a very notable work by H. Teichmann.

It may seem presumptuous to compare processes in the atmosphere with phenomena of organic development. But let us listen to the words of a professional meteorologist. In his book "Dynamik der Zyklonen", P. Raethjen speaks about the regions of low pressure (cyclones) in the following way: The cyclone "has a typical life history with characteristic phases, its origin, development and the way it dies away. It reproduces itself not as the propagation of a wave in space, but—behaving like a living creature—through the '*birth*' of a young 'frontal cyclone' out of the womb ('frontal zone') of an adult 'central cyclone'. (By central cyclone is meant the great stationary regions of low pressure. Author's note.) . . . Only we must not forget that this 'dying and becoming' is an *essential* characteristic of cyclones". And again: ". . . As the atmosphere behaves like a living creature, it is only fair to consider and treat it as a '*whole*'. Questions which cannot be understood on their own will, if taken as a whole, harmonise *together*."—Even earlier than this, well-known meteorologists drew attention to the *biological* language which the weather men are continually being forced to use.

The rhythms of the above-mentioned trains of vortices in the atmosphere have their own particular laws. The creation of vortices, i.e. regions of low pressure, is a process that follows an annual course with high and low points. According to A. Schmauss, who in a whole lifetime of daily weather observations was able to form a picture of these laws, which he also worked out mathematically, the "dynamic year" begins on 29th September with a low in the activity of the atmosphere. By activity in the atmosphere he means the meteorological movements which occur between Northern England and France. This is measured by the difference in pressure between these two geographical regions in Western Europe.

With the beginning of the dynamic year on 29th September an impulse is created which leads the activity of the atmosphere to a climax which is reached, on an average over many years, on 9th January. The activity then decreases again to its lowest point at the end of May or the beginning of June, after this it rises once more and remains high, though varying rhythmically, till 15th September, whence it then sinks down until 29th September. There the new impulse of a growing activity begins again, leading up to the climax in January. Thus, the great rise and fall of the regions of high and low pressure in the "breathing of the continents" is rhythmically differentiated still more delicately, like a language or a symphony. Schmauss says of this: "For the meteorologist, who is acquainted

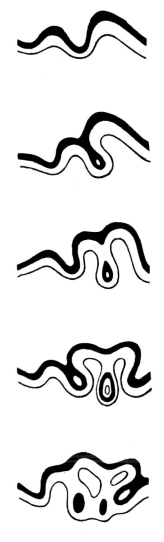

Isolation of cold air pockets (after Rossby)

with these things, this calendar of the change in the great bodies of air over the continents has the significance of an orchestral score, which indicates when each instrument should come in. Of course, any instrument can miss its entry: even so, it is a great joy to know the score."

The important stages in the rhythm of the dynamic year will be seen to correspond with the main festivals of the Christian year. Easter lies in the rhythmical events of the seasons between winter and summer, in the battle between the extremes and is therefore not very prominent as a single event, as a "singularity". But Whitsun, which falls according to Easter, and has a moveable date, is conspicuous in the course of the dynamic year. Between 20th May and the beginning of June there is a moment of least activity in the atmosphere, a moment which, like Whitsun, does not occur at a fixed date but belongs to this whole stretch of time. Then follows the autumn festival of Michaelmas and then Christmas, which was originally celebrated on 6th January, very near to the singular moment of 9th January, when there is a climax of atmospheric activity. Among the conspicuous points, which have at least a tendency to recur during the course of the year, there are, for instance, the well-known days of frost in May, the cold spell between 2nd and 20th June and the thundery period around Ascension Day.

What do such events in the formation of weather and clouds really mean? The realisation that these rhythms are extra terrestrial is becoming increasingly widespread. The sequence of cyclones is today considered to be connected with events on the sun, and these, for instance solar activity (sun spots), are considered to be due to the effect on the sun of the interweaving movements of the planets. May not the great cosmic events in the universe have their effect in the "sensitive" surfaces of contact in the atmospheric mantle of our earth? The laws of the heavens address themselves to these membranes as though speaking into delicate ears. Organs are created, and the earth, with its oceans and continents and its landscapes, becomes a great organism. The earth, like a living creature, is received into the still greater living community of the celestial world. If it were possible to look down on land and sea from a great height, we would be able to experience the creation of vortices in the belts of low pressure through the confluence of different masses of air. Where different streams of air meet, waves arise along the surface of contact and then curl in; this all happens in enormous dimensions over the continents and oceans. Sometimes one single such "vortex" has the dimensions of a whole continent.

On the earth we do not experience these spacious movements; we only notice the daily ups and downs of the weather as it passes. Great processes like the battle between different masses of air, for instance, between cold, polar air and warm, humid sea air streaming in from the south, appear to us as the varied, dramatic events of our daily weather. A visible expression of these processes taking place

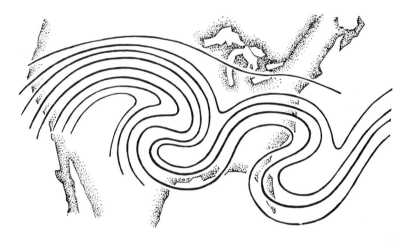

Train of vortices over the U.S.A.
(after Wexler and Namias)

above us is the formation and dissolution of the clouds and the varied kinds of precipitation, which dictate the character of the weather. We have here not only movements which through their interplay create moving forms, but there also occur differences in temperature, and connected with these, the expansion and contraction of the air and the release and absorption of water. This last process is the main incentive for meteorological events, because in it large quantities of heat are absorbed or released, according to the ruling of the celestial universe, which plays its part in the process.

The vagaries of the weather are a play with the intermingling of water in the atmosphere. It absorbs great quantities of heat in the warm regions of the earth and either carries this warmth to more northerly latitudes in the form of warm currents in the oceans, or as water vapour in the great air currents of the planet. Where the water meets with cold air it separates out again like a warm breath

in the cold winter air, and becomes visible as mist, cloud or precipitation. In this way it releases the great quantities of heat which it had absorbed in warmer regions. As soon as the water becomes visible, the warmth it has collected earlier, and usually elsewhere, issues forth again.

So once more we see in water a mediator and balancer between contrasts; it takes what is superfluous at one place and bears it over great distances to where it is needed. Water as the bearer of warmth acts as a great regulator of the gain and loss of heat of the planet. The visible expression of this are the clouds and the weather with all its different elements of pressure, temperature, humidity, wind and so on.

Where in the atmosphere warmth pours forth out of the condensing water vapour, it immediately causes ascending currents to arise in the air. It is not necessarily always over warm land that air ascends. Ascending winds can arise in the air itself if water condenses into clouds, thus releasing warmth in the midst of the air. The air will then rise up; the higher it rises the more it cools, releasing more water in the form of clouds. Still more warmth is thus freed, causing the air to rise still higher. This continued process results in the familiar upwelling cloud formations we see in the summer (Plate

71), gathering and towering up to form thunder clouds. It is simply the interplay of flowing currents, in which the most varied, consistently changing cloud formations arise, reminiscent of animal or organic shapes. The basic principle of organic formation, as we have learned to recognise it, appears here in all its variety of possibilities. Many of the elements of form and movement which we described in connection with water can be found again in connection with the formation of clouds. Waves and rhythmically arranged ridge formations arise when the wind blows across a thin layer of cloud (Plate 73), curling vortices arise at the moving edge of clouds (Plate 75); there are sources and sinks and great and small spiralling surfaces. The little tufts of alto-cumulus or cirro-cumulus clouds, for instance, show where there is an upwelling current. Air rises in each little flake of cloud and falls again at its edge. A great variety of small air circulations spreads out in a field of "fleecy" clouds. If a wind arises which drives the whole field onwards, they arrange themselves in rows, turn into scales that seem to push over one another like ice floes in a river, and create forms that are familiar to us from the varied kinds of ridges and ribs made by water in sand.

We shall refrain from going into all these forms in detail. It will suffice to say that they all arise from movements which we have to a large extent already met with in water.

The previous pages have been concerned with the interplay of water and air and have stressed what they have in common. In the following it will be our task to characterise their differences.

There are many similar characteristics in the streaming movements of water and air; but the faster air moves the more its own nature asserts itself. It becomes compressible and can thus expand or contract, becoming less or more dense. It can do this because of the elasticity and compressibility that are characteristic of its nature. Water cannot be noticeably compressed until it has turned into steam, a condition in which it resembles air. And as the nature of air, its elasticity, only asserts itself when the air is travelling at great speed, it may be presumed that it is essentially in the nature of air to flow faster than water. This is indeed the case. Even the speed of moderate winds greatly exceeds that of flowing water, and even at slower speeds air has to flow much faster—about fourteen times as fast—in order to cause vortex trains to arise on the same scale as those in water. The tendency to greater speeds, to great variations in volume, its ability to expand and contract and thus alter its density, are characteristics of the element of air. But all these processes in the air are accompanied by changes in heat; the air reacts immediately with expansion or contraction to any change in temperature. In this it manifests a kind of "sensitivity", and thus passes on any tiny shock or impulse in rhythmical expansion or contraction, imparting it to the air spaces around. Every increase or decrease in density is accompanied by a delicate heat process; there takes place a corresponding decrease or increase in temperature. Every sound wave moving through the air bears with it a delicate, rhythmical heat process.

In the way in which it expands and contracts, *air* seems to be three dimensional. And *water* with its formation of great inner and outer surfaces is two dimensional and planar. This fact finds expression in the breathing processes of living creatures. In creatures which inhabit the water, these breathing processes are entirely adjusted to the formation of great flat surfaces; in the creatures of the air, however, the element of rhythmical expansion and contraction is added. The elasticity of the lungs and chest are the expression of the properties of the air.

The phenomenon of bird migration, though not directly taking the form of an expanding and contracting breathing process, can lead to a deeper understanding of the nature of air.

Many birds flock together in the autumn and fly to warmer lands. Sometimes they proceed in great crowds, sometimes in small groups, some of them in strict formation. It is as though each of these groups were to become a complete whole; this is indeed the case. What happens when they fly together in this way; when for instance they form a triangle open on one side, or a slanting line, or fly in what looks like a disorderly flock?

These questions have been answered by the interesting though unfortunately little known results of research carried out by R. Schieferstein. Schieferstein discovered that birds flying in an arrow or wedge formation are linked together through the air connecting them, or rather through the elasticity of the air. The flock of birds in triangle formation is a totality and to this totality belongs the air which bears it. The flock moves in an *aerial form* which it creates for itself as a whole, but which has an effect on each individual bird.

A comparison will serve to make this clear. It can be observed how a swan swimming on a pond draws behind it a wedge-shaped wake on which the cygnets sometimes swim. A wedge-shaped formation like this may be seen in the wake of every ship. On an expedition to Africa, Idrac observed how the natives of the Gold Coast make use of these waves. They row in their small canoes behind the coastal steamer until they have reached its speed, then place themselves on

The boats of the natives perch on the waves in the wake of a steamer and are carried along by them (after Idrac)

the forward facing slope of a wave on which, as they are moving with the same speed, they can ride as though on a slanting plane and be carried along without any great effort. The little boats lie one on each wave in the steamer's wake, which splays out backwards in a wedge-shaped formation.

This is a picture of the flight of birds in migration. Each bird lies on a "wave" which is made in the air by the leader. The beats of their wings follow the ups and downs of the wave and simply make visible what, as a vibrating aerial form, surrounds and bears them all in the arrow formation. By studying the wing positions of the birds flying in arrow formation, Schieferstein was able to deduce the actual shape of the form. Each bird flies in a fixed position in the aerial form, and the form itself unites all the individual birds. A bird does not need much strength, for it is as though the movement of the wave of air were to raise and lower its wings for it. If one of the birds has an excess of energy, it will do more than simply allow itself to be carried along. With the beating of its wings it will strengthen the whole wave, will infuse the aerial form with energy, from which all will benefit who would on their own account no longer have the strength to fly. These take energy from the whole moving field of air. Indeed, even the leading bird itself draws energy from this field. Schieferstein says: "The current error, that the bird flying at the apex of the triangle has to work considerably harder than those following it, must be corrected. The wave of the field of airstreams, created reciprocally by all the separate birds, spreads out in space with the speed of sound and therefore, as the speed at which the birds fly is much slower, it precedes them considerably, so that the leading bird can if necessary take energy from the field just as can all the others."

The arrow formation is a totality in which the separate birds lie embedded like organs. A new body has been created out of air in which, as with the body of sound of an orchestra, the single instrument to a great extent merges into the whole; it is, however, a necessary part of the whole. The separate birds are linked together by the surrounding air as though by elastic threads.

Schieferstein says of this: "We may imagine the separate birds linked together for instance through invisible elastic threads. If a bird uses more energy than would be necessary for its propulsion through the air, it tightens the threads which link it to its surroundings and thus imparts to the whole formation its excessive energy of propulsion. . . . If on the other hand a bird has less energy than is necessary to propel it along within the formation, a tension in the opposite direction arises in the connecting elastic links, and the bird, whose movements lag behind the movement of the whole field . . . receives from it the energy necessary to its propulsion along with the others."

The air, which connects the birds like an elastic medium, acts like a muscle. It unites the different limbs of the formation into a unity which was not there before and is caused to do this by a higher being, namely, the group soul of these birds. One might almost say that this group soul manifests itself in the density of air and acts as an integrating muscular system. The elastic properties of muscles are indeed similar to the elasticity of the air. In a muscle these properties of air are simply embodied and made visible in matter. Thus it comes about that, during a long flight over many hundreds of miles, each single bird, "elastically" connected with the whole flight, beats its wings exactly as many times as all the others in the formation. The entire process is an aerial form, an organic whole moving through the air. — The bird is a creature of the air; it is born out of the air and entrusts itself to it. It cannot possibly be abandoned by the air.

Schieferstein was also able to show how even in a seemingly dis-organised flock, every bird flies along connected with the whole, beating its wings the same number of times during the course of a long flight as all the other birds in the same flock.

Observation of the wings of a bird in flight will once again reveal the form of the spiralling surface. Indeed, flapping flight seems only to be possible through the twisting and turning of the wing about its longitudinal axis in certain phases of its movements; a form of movement which, as we have seen, belongs to the nature and characteristics of movements in flowing media.

There are various winged plant seeds which picture in their form single phases out of a sequence of movements in the flight of birds. They are to be found in plants which entrust their seeds to the air and let them fly away. In the movements of flight of such plant forms are to be seen many of the archetypal movements mentioned in the course of these descriptions.

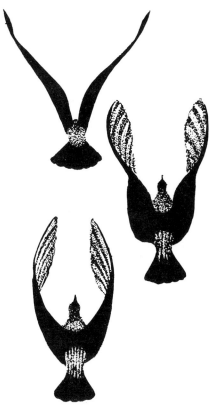

Phases in the flight of a bird (after Guidi)

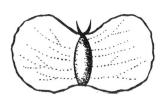

Single phases of the flight of birds are captured in the forms of airborne seeds (after R. Schmidt)

Whirling path of air in the organ pipe,
often to be found in the formation of joints
(after Eidmann)

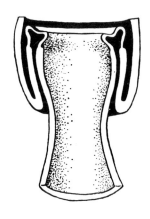

A glance at some of the formations found in the insect world will reveal how insects, too, know how to utilise the air. They incorporate in their bodies the streaming forms of air, consolidating the movement outside and around them into a permanent form. In their joints there are vortex formations; in their wings, more or less marked, spiralling membranes; and in the formation of the limbs, first the intucking and then the unfurling of the surfaces between regions of growth of different speeds in the chrysalis. With their feelers and the bristles of their wings they comb the air, dispersing it into tiny delicate curling surfaces. An inconceivable stream of minute vortex trains passes over the surface of their wings and it is as though the air were to take on a settled form in the countless little scales and flakes on the wings' surfaces. Arranged down to the last detail of the most delicate lamelli and layers, as though in a small cosmic vortex system, these wing membranes give off the colourful shimmer of the butterflies, those creatures which are the embodiment of air and light.

Another important fact is that many of the processes just described are at the same time audible ones, revealing something of their actual inner nature by giving off sounds. In them, as opposed to the world of water, something new arises in our field of experience; it is the world of sounds inasmuch as the sounds are the expression of animated creatures. In the voices of the animals, for instance of the birds, the world of the soul itself begins to sound. The whole world of sound is alive in the atmosphere and creates for itself audible expression in the voices and noises of the animals.

Joint formations in insects
(from Eidmann, after Weber)

When a breeze blows through a deciduous or a coniferous wood, it is parted by every leaf, every pine needle, closing again behind it while forming the most delicate vortex trains. A feature of the life of the wood is the fact that as well as the great surfaces formed by its leaves, corresponding "leaves" are formed in the air by the wind, like trailers behind the real leaves. Every leaf, every pine needle gives rise to one of the dividing surfaces we have so often described. A similar thing happens when a bird or butterfly or other insect flies through the air; endless surfaces are ceaselessly being created in the air. Just imagine the surface formations made by insects as they hover and dart about on a summer's day. At every moment an invisible "field of leaves" made of air arises and dies away, engraved momentarily in the air by the tiny wings of the insects. It consists of innumerable lamelli which are in themselves still further divided into vortices through the feelers and the bristles on the front edges of the insects' wings. When the air is opened up into all these many inner surfaces, it is as though it were permeated through and through by a delicate sensitivity. Indeed, it is so. Air thus combed through and filled with humming vibration is indeed sensitive. A "body of air" like this may often be seen when a swarm of little midges dances in the air on a summer evening. In a cloud of insects the air is divided up into great surfaces by the rapid beating of their wings. In this way a body of air becomes sensitive. If one hums or whistles a series of notes, it is possible to see how the whole swarm may be influenced, as though by an invisible hand, by a particular note in the series. At one moment it may stretch out lengthwise, at the next widen, or be wafted away or drawn nearer, as though by an invisible wave. The air and the swarm of insects unite to form *one* body, into which the individual insect merges like a cell in an organism.

Sensitive aerial formation may also be created experimentally by allowing a thin layer of air to stream into still air through a slit. This thin layer of air corresponds to the incision made by the wing of an insect. The insect cuts a narrow incision in the air along which waves and vortices form. The thin layer of air coming out of a slit— itself made of air—behaves like just such an incision made in the air, as though by an insect or leaf; it creates friction with the surrounding still air, forming waves and vortices. The wall of the slit may be regarded as an obstacle, taking into account that the needles on the branch of a pine tree, through which the wind blows, form many slits between them, while at the same time each needle is also an obstacle. But a slit may be regarded as an obstacle also because, for the air streaming through it, it is a defile, causing increased resistance, and so we again meet the same phenomenon as in water: a stream flowing around an obstacle or through a slit creates similar trains of vortices, only with the separate vortices spinning in opposite directions.

Instead of air it is also possible to allow combustible gas to stream out of the slit, which makes the inner processes more easily visible and also offers certain advantages in photographing them. This method was used above all by P. E. Schiller, who has made a thorough study of flames that are sensitive to sound. Every vibration in the air, every sound imprints itself on such sensitive streams and forms their inner structure, just as a cloud of midges can be influenced by sounds. Plates 67–70 show the forms which arise through the effect on the sensitive flames of the same note played on different musical instruments. Each instrument has its own quality of tone, which is expressed visibly by these forms of movement. We must realise that in general every note of an instrument consists of a number of separate notes, fundamental tones and overtones, which give it its special character, and it is this special character that impresses itself in its individual nature on the flame.

We also recognise the speech of a man by its quality of tone, which is an expression of his personal individuality in soul and spirit (Plates 62–66). And so via his voice and its quality of tone his individuality impresses itself on the flame when he speaks. It is as though the flame were a delicate sense organ like an ear. But one could also say that the organ of hearing, especially the internal ear, is a kind of sensitive flame, translated into the watery element and sensitive to sound. The flowing, wavy lamella of the flame corresponds to the basilar membrane in the internal ear, which under the influence of sounds also forms waves and creates vortices on both sides of itself. The image of the sensitive dividing surface, with its series of vortices on either side, is to be seen once more, this time in the internal ear. According to the pitch of the note, the train of vortices in the ear is more marked in the lower, middle or upper region. High notes cause it to arise low down, near the fenestra ovalis; with low notes it appears at the end of the basilar membrane, near the apex of the cochlea (see the chapter on: The Ear). This phenomenon may be found in the sensitive flame. If it is influenced by high notes it grows shorter and becomes formed particularly at its base, and if it is affected by low notes it stretches in length and reaches upwards.

The whole band of lamelli in such flames is twisted about itself, just as is the basilar membrane of the internal ear. They are both curled, right from the start, like a twisted strip of paper held at both ends. Furthermore, the spiralling, streaming band of flame grows wider towards the top, just as the basilar membrane of the internal ear widens towards the apex of the cochlea. (Added to this twist, in the band of the basilar membrane there is also a spiral twist.) We shall not here attempt to describe in detail how the internal ear resembles a flame which is sensitive to sound. What has been hinted at so far will suffice for the further progress of our considerations. What has been said is enough to show that great and small worlds resonate together. The streaming processes which take place on a huge scale in the vast vortex trains of the atmosphere, with their fronts forming widespread sensitive surfaces, are repeated in the tiny formations of the internal ear of the human being. In these the world of sound becomes audible. It is the same world of sound as when the harmony of the spheres in the great universe plays upon the membranes of the atmospheric fronts. "Nought is within, nought is without, for what is within is also without."

An essential factor in the sensitivity of such streams of air is the measure of the speed of flow. The highest sensitivity is reached in the experiment when the stream of air begins to make a rushing sound, that is, when it is split up into countless microscopically small vortices, as is the case with a sensitive swarm of insects. Then it is that the world of sound, like a superior power, can play on it from outside. The sound then becomes visible as a moving form. We have met with something similar in the cosmic qualities of water, where the superior powers of the harmonies of the spheres have transformed the inner quality of the moving water. In the one and in the other we experience the fact that the mobile element, be it air or water, becomes sensitive, thus creating an instrument for a superior being. Wherever such sensitivity arises, it comes about through *movement*. It is the movement which prepares the way for a creative event. The field has to be ploughed and the sod turned and opened up in order to be able to receive the seed.

Sensitive flames or streams of air react to every sound; they also react to the human voice. With its infinite possibilities of variation,

Train of vortices in an organ pipe (after Carrière)

121

Streams of air meeting at various angles (after Carrière)

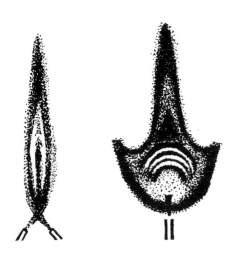

the human voice can affect these flames in manifold ways. Speech is seen to be an actual creator of forms in the air.

These experiments using a stream of air that is sensitive to sound can be varied, by placing a small obstacle in the path of the stream. This splits the air into two streams, which unite again beyond the obstacle. Or instead of using an obstacle, two streams of air can be arranged so that they meet at a more or less acute or obtuse angle (Carrière). In both cases waves or trains of vortices of such great speed arise, that they begin to emit a sound, reacting in their turn on the sensitive stream of air. In an interplay of this kind complicated forms arise, which demonstrate still more clearly the laws of the air. We shall not be surprised to see forms appearing similar to those found in the world of birds and insects. After all, in birds and insects the very laws of the air have become solidified in the forms of their bodies, and in all their actions these animals cannot but manifest the laws of the air. Even the way in which they build and create for themselves an outward protection speaks in the end of their origin in the region of the air. Their constructions are an expression of movement come to rest and of the element out of which they have been created. But the great variety of possibilities shows also that each of them is a single entity in its own right. Nature in her abundance has condensed and solidified each one individually, a one-sided manifestation of infinite possibilities.

To sum up: the flame which is sensitive to sound makes visible how the air is ready to receive every formative impulse that works in it or comes towards it. The more varied the formative impulse, the greater the variety of form in the moving air or flame. Of all the possibilities Nature has for producing sound, the human voice and speech have the greatest range of variations. All the forms that have up to now been described may be reproduced here through the effects of speech. Does not Nature here point to speech as the source of all her great abundance of forms?

Something of the nature of the elements is revealed in their arrangement in the order of solid, liquid and gaseous layers. The solid element lies lowest as a foundation; its surface is to a great extent covered by the watery element; and above that rises the atmosphere, which gradually becomes lost in universal space. The solid element belongs entirely to the earth, while the air is almost completely freed from it; water maintains a balance between the two. Wherever water is active, it tries to bring the solid and the gaseous into its own sphere by breaking up and dissolving solids and by absorbing gases. Water even goes out into the spaces of air, permeating the air and uniting it with the earth through all that takes place in the meteorological events. The close interrelationship between the ever-present element of water with the earth on the one hand and air on the other, makes it necessary to undertake a very conscious and detailed study of air, if we are really to understand it according to its own nature.

We have already met with a characteristic feature in the behaviour of the elements, namely, their relation to movement, whereas air subjects itself to the most intensive movement, the solid element remains entirely stationary. Again, water takes the middle way, avoiding the rapid motion of air and maintaining a measured speed. Very great speeds, forced upon it for instance if it is caused to fall through a pipe, are foreign to its nature. In nature, falling water dissolves into droplets and mist and floats gently to the ground. Water forced into excessive speed vaporises and begins to obey the laws of the flow of air; for it is air whose nature it is to move at great speeds. In the great range of possibilities which the air has between the resting state and very fast motion lies its propensity to quick and intense change. It is in the very nature of water ceaselessly to repeat the same pattern at the same place, perhaps behind a stone in a stream. Air on the other hand must always be doing something new. Often quite capriciously, it will change the direction and force of its movement, expressing in the element of wind and weather its whimsical and constantly changing activity.

The air responds spontaneously with marked expansion or contraction to every minute increase or decrease in temperature. With these expansions and contractions the air also undergoes a change in material density, whereby it becomes lighter or heavier and thus rises or falls in the atmosphere. This rhythm is like a breathing which flows through the whole atmospheric mantle of the earth. We have already met with it on the large scale in the process of the "breathing of the continents". In the breathing process, air meets with the forces of soul. Thus, air may become a "body" for soul forces.

On the smallest scale, too, air is able to vibrate in the delicate rhythms of its increase and decrease in density, whereby it becomes the bearer of the world of sound. It is a process which, like the changeability of the atmosphere, bears within it a great range of possibilities. What an abundance of sounds and noises comes forth from nature, not to mention the possibilities given to mankind in music and speech. Do not sounds and noises, and indeed every voice, reveal something of the inmost nature of the creatures uttering them? How differently are we affected by the howling winds of a gale, by the jubilation of a lark on the wing, by the chirping of the crickets on a summer's night. Every creature utters sounds according to its nature; every sound reveals the inmost processes of its soul. It is an inner world which reveals itself here, a world of moods of soul, which become manifest in the reverberating air.

The soul forces of the air reveal themselves not only in the world of sound but also in light and colour. Great are the variations possible in the atmosphere in the play of colour at sunrise or sunset, and how the colours vary in the drama of the weather! When we enter the world of sounds, of the play of colours and even of meteorology, we meet in fact with soul processes. It is as though the laws of the world of sound and colour, even of meteorology, had become densified through the activity of air, into the creatures of the air—the birds and insects. Something of its very nature sounds forth from them or becomes visible in the play of colour.

Any naturalist knows how closely the creatures of the air are connected with the events of the weather. They partake in the great seasonal breathing of the atmosphere as well as in the rise and fall of the air-flow over the countryside. They actually form a part of the soul of the countryside. We have seen, in the phenomenon of bird migration and in insects, how the laws of the air are expressed even in the structure of their bodies. They vibrate according to the laws of the air; the elasticity of muscles is the elasticity of the air projected into the visible world. The soul of the animal plays equally upon its body and upon the air. Air becomes soul-bearing substance.

The elements of the earth are arranged in a certain order; it is the same order as that in which the spirit descends into matter and can clothe itself in a body. Out of the world of the celestial laws of the eternal mathematical ordering of the stars, which makes itself manifest in the audible harmony of numbers in the world of sound, the spirit descends into the silence of water, there to be revealed in the ordering of number and substance in organic form. The laws of the stars descend and, through the mediating elements of air and water, impress themselves upon the earth.

"O Man, speak, and the source and life of the universe shall be revealed through thee." Rudolf Steiner

In the course of our considerations we have been led further and further through the abundance of natural phenomena to recognise that there is something spiritual expressed in them. With the use of many examples we have attempted to show how forms arise out of the gaseous or liquid elements, but above all how it is to *movement* that we must ascribe these forms. They are the movements of a spiritually living being descending from the world of cosmic laws to take on bodily form through the circulations of air and water. At all stages of this descent, movement as such has constantly shown itself to be the *tool* used by a world of *being* working in upon the elements.

If we observe how in embryonic development an organism is gradually created out of the liquid, our attention is drawn to movements which play their part in fashioning it according to invisible plans, though they are themselves not all visible in the finished form. They are like the hands of the potter in their abundance of possibilities, moulding a vessel from without and within and then withdrawing again into the invisible world. They are movements which originate in the will and spirit of a living being. As movements they are actually the creative and formative forces through which the idea underlying the forms can be impressed on the elements. Once this has been accomplished, the creative movement releases the form and appears in it as a *function*, of which the embodied being may now make use.

The human larynx is one of the most beautiful examples of this. All the moving forms which we have seen in the course of these considerations may be found again in the possibilities of movement of the human larynx. This means that all the movements which Nature uses in the creation of her creatures and also all those movements which, once created, the creatures may use, may be found in the human larynx—as though in a great gathering of creative beings. The larynx has innumerable possibilities of movement, and with every one of them it can delicately influence the stream of breath and impress moving forms upon the flow of air, which then become audible for us as sounds, tones, speech.

Examine the structure of the larynx and its adjacent organs. It is obvious that in its differentiated forms it is not so much the resting form which is significant as the moving form with its immense possibilities of variation. This is expressed in the way the numerous joints and groups of muscles are co-ordinated in a great variety of ways. The significance of all these joint and muscle actions can be understood if we realise that in their interplay these movements serve to mould the stream of air and form it into the stream of speech. For the stream of air is obstructed by a great variety of forms: narrowing slits, elastic membranes, pouches, spiralling curves—obstacles of the most varied form, elasticity and plasticity (vocal cords, epiglottis, soft palate, uvula, tongue, teeth, lips and so on). Each of these moulds the stream of air and forms it in a particular way; all together they can impress upon it an endless variety of shapes and forms.

We have met with the sensitive stream of air which arises when air emerges through a narrow slit. A corresponding phenomenon may be found in the larynx, where the stream of air issuing from the lungs has to pass through the slit between the vocal cords. The stream causes these to vibrate and the vibrations immediately work back on it, dividing it up rhythmically and becoming the source of the audible sound. Through the further moulding of the stream of air, in the interplay of the adjacent organs, further formation of the

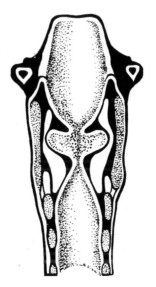

Diagram of the human larynx

sound takes place. According to the varying shapes made by the *cavities* of the mouth and throat, so the sound is altered and becomes the many different tones and over-tones of the voice. Some of these are magnified into fundamental tones, others are suppressed, whereby the most varied timbres arise. We experienced these differentiated tones as the characteristic vowels, their origin is where the stream of air is restricted and has to pass the vocal cords. Furthermore, with palate, tongue, teeth and lips the human being can mould the stream of air in such a way as to produce the consonants.

It is at the vocal cords that the whole soul life of a man flows into the formation of the stream of speech, the soul's means of expression. The as yet unformed stream of air issues forth from the region of the will; at the vocal cords it receives the impulses which come from the conscious soul life of the human being, striving to communicate with the outer world (articulation). As yet unformed, the air coming from the lung enters the larynx. It leaves the organs of speech structured in finest detail—in waves, vibrations and vortices; definite, though ever-changing formations. Their richly varied interplay builds complicated forms out of the fundamental, archetypal movements of the streaming air.[1]

The delicate vibrations which mould the sensitive flame through the elasticity of the air have their counterpart in the larynx in the delicate vibrations of soul life. The soul uses the elasticity of the vocal cords like an instrument on which to play. Here, the instrument which influences the sensitive flame from a distance has entered directly into the walls of the slit. The soul of the human being allows its inner abundance of tension and relaxation, sympathy and antipathy to play on the elastic vocal cords, stretching or relaxing, lengthening or shortening them, narrowing or widening the slit. Accordingly they vibrate in fast or slow rhythms. In the same way it is the soul of the human being which activates the interplay of the adjacent organs.

We have already pointed out how the air can be the bearer of soul forces and how it is particularly its elasticity which, like a tool, can be used by the soul as it expands and contracts in sympathy and antipathy. In the larynx we see a wonderful co-operation in this triad of air, soul and elasticity. The delicate interplay of the elasticity

---

[1] All these descriptions refer to the formation of sound as such and not to the content of what is spoken.

of the air is solidified to a visible form in the elasticity of the vocal cords and the groups of muscles in the larynx. The riches of the inner life of a human being become as it were physically graspable; airy forms are constantly being born in the larynx.

It is possible to observe these forms of air if single phases of this constantly changing play of movement in the larynx are made visible in a suitable experimental arrangement, outside the human larynx. As air and water have certain features in common, the quick movements of the air may be transposed into the slower movements of water, as long as certain rules are observed.

If water or air is allowed to issue from a slit, vortex trains arise, with which we are familiar (Plate 24). Similar trains of vortices may be created by drawing a small rod through water or air. A single such vortex train will of course correspond in the larynx only to the most simple form of sound, caused by *one* particular position of the organs of speech (Plate 29). But even the same sound uttered *several* times will change the form of the air; the same impulse is again and again inserted into the formation of air which has already been created (Plate 31). If impulses of *different* kinds and strengths (corresponding to the vowels and consonants of a word) follow on one another at short intervals, more complicated forms will arise accordingly (Plate 32).

We may recall that the interplay of the most varied streams and moulding movements is necessary in order to create the form of even a simple organ. This will help us to understand that in the organ of speech, with its constant variations of movement, a great variety of organ-like forms are created out of the air. We may here behold with our very eyes the way in which forms issue forth from the word. In Plate 32 we see how many small forms, all in a flowing relationship with one another, are incorporated like organs in a great, rhythmically arranged form. It is like a picture of the invisible streaming forces which weave an organism and its separate organs into a whole. Even though these formations are at a very simple stage, they show something of the rich variety of possibilities inherent in movements working together. (See also Plates 29–32.)

The variety of formations which Nature and the human larynx allow to stream forth must be infinitely great! As man unites all Nature's formative possibilities in his own human form, he is able to bring forth from his larynx not only all the single organic forms of nature but also a union of them all. This means that the human being unites in his organs of speech all the formative movements by which

Sagittal section through the speech organs of the human being (after Corning)

he has been created. And so within man another man, a moving human being, is at work.

It is the secret of the biblical story of the Creation that Adam is able to utter the names of all creatures and things and also his own name —the mystery of man himself. He can do so because the Godhead first inspired him with living forming forces—the breath of life— forming him according to them. The creative word of the universe itself, original movement of spirit, formed him and his larynx; now it again sounds forth from him in creative forms. No wonder that these laws are to be found in the larynx!

In the arrangement of the organs of human speech, as they are drawn in the accompanying sketch, is revealed once more the archetypal gesture of all living, streaming movement; it is pictured here in solid organic form. "Every time that a man speaks he produces out of himself something of that creative element which existed in the ancient days of creation, when the human being was moulded out of cosmic depths, out of ethereal realms, into an airy form, before he acquired a fluid form and, later still, his solid earthly body. Every time we speak, we transport ourselves back into the evolution of the universe and man as it was in primeval ages . . ." (from a lecture held by R. Steiner on 24th June, 1924).

The stream of speech, like a flaming sword, pours forth from man, announcing the inner secret of his creation. It is the "sensitive flame", issuing forth from the region of the will, on which man can impress his moods—the "meteorology" of his soul. But he also communicates this to his surroundings, which take it in through the activity of listening; it is recreated in the receptive processes of the organ of hearing. The sensitive flame is the underlying concept both of the larynx and of the organ of hearing. In both it is the creative principle—an "organ" not as yet brought to the resting state of form, but retaining its functional quality as pure movement. It functions in the intermediate region where forms are for ever being created; with its delicate sensitive boundary surface, it is a portal through which all the imponderable forces may enter into the world of earthly substance.

We have come to know the sensitive boundary surfaces on a large scale in the weather fronts with their accompanying heat processes. They are the organs of hearing that listen to what comes from the cosmic universe; at the same time they are the organs of speech through which the starry universe expresses itself, in a manner which is coloured by the moody nature of the earthly sphere. As on a small scale in the larynx, so also in these gigantic speech organs, forms are created, which, on a grand scale, contain all the possibilities of creation. In man these creative possibilities are united in a streaming together of the creative word of the universe. "All things were made by the Word, and without the Word was not any thing made that was made."

We have as yet only spoken in general about many possibilities of movement, but we will now call them by their true names. In the abundance of possible movements in the organ of speech, certain ever-repeated characteristic archetypal movements, which we know as the vowels and consonants, can be singled out. As characteristic elements of movement they remain unaltered throughout the languages of all time. Indeed, it is out of these fundamental gestures or sound-movements, which have a spiritual origin, that the manifold movements of the larnyx arise in the first place, and it is these archetypal movements of the vowels and consonants that give birth to all manner of forms. The true name of a thing is pronounced, when the form-creating, archetypal gestures of the consonants really do create the thing as a moving form.

There is nothing in nature that cannot be created and named by speech, for in naming a thing, man, through his speech, creates it anew as a form in the space of air, in so far as his words still partake of the living origin of language. Everything surrounding us in nature has a part in the original gestures, but only a part. Man, uniting all nature, has at his disposal the whole—a whole alphabet.

In olden times the archetypal gestures were experienced each in its own one-sided aspect; the gestures of certain cosmic forces were seen in images of animal forms. The world of consonants was arranged as a zodiac; the vowels represented the moving world of the planets. The spoken word is more than the intellectual naming of a thing, more than a "nomen"; it is form-creating, spiritual reality.

If the larynx bears within it all the archetypal gestures of the world of the stars which lead to the human form, if, in other words, it contains over again a whole man as a moving form, then only a small step further is needed to the thought that the archetypal gestures may not only be made audible, through the larynx, but also visible, through the whole moving human form. This would lead to an art of movement which uses the moving human being as a means of expression according to the laws of the universal alphabet through which he was born out of the cosmos. This new art, the art of eurythmy, together with a revival of the art of speech based on the same cosmic background, has been created by Rudolf Steiner. In eurythmy the manifold movements of the ethereal archetypal gestures are made visible through the whole human form; they are the basic gestures of the physical larynx which mould the stream of air.

As well as speech, man also bears within him the world of tones, of music. These, too, he can make visible according to their laws through the movement of his human form. Speech and eurythmy are in the end the same experience, one auditory, the other visual. Man and the world have been created by speech—the eurythmy of spiritually creative beings. Speech and eurythmy are given to man because he is himself to become creative in spirit.

"The human being as he stands before us is a completed form. But this form has been created out of movement. It has arisen from archetypal forms which were continually taking shape and passing away again. Movement does not proceed from quiescence; on the contrary, that which is in a state of rest originates in movement. In eurythmy we are reaching back to primordial movement.

What is it that my Creator, working out of original, cosmic being, does in me as a man?

If you would give me the answer to this question you must make movements of eurythmy. God makes eurythmy movements, and as the result of His eurythmy there arises the form of man. . . ." (From a lecture given by Rudolf Steiner on 24th June, 1924.)

Whether we speak of streaming water or moving air, of the formation of organs or the movements of the human form, of speech, of eurythmy or of the regulating movements of the stars, it is all one: the archetypal gesture of the cosmic alphabet, the word of the universe, which uses the element of movement in order to bring forth nature and man.

Afterword

Forms of Flow in Art

It has been our aim to show how Nature reproduces in all manner of ways all the forms and elements of movement appertaining to the human being. The opposite is also true. All movements and forms that the universe holds in readiness meet in Man and are thus united at a higher level. Moreover, in speech, through which he differs from all the rest of creation, Man can let go forth from himself, like an echo, these same forms and elements of movement. What he is and what sounds forth from him is an echo of the glory of the creative Word of the universe itself. Therefore in the days when this open secret could still be experienced, speech was held sacred. Only in special places was it permissible to use, practise and communicate something of the power of speech. Not until later did it lose its creative force and become merely a means of communication. Today we know hardly anything of this power of speech; what was practised secretly in the sacred temples has echoed away into silence. In a few works of art here and there a remnant has been handed down to us, from which we can guess how deeply the forces of the "creative, formative Word of the universe" entered intimately into the life of the peoples. In these works of art are to be found many of the forms we have been contemplating here.

Plate 81 depicts the threshold stone of an initiation chamber of the Bronze Age in Ireland (Newgrange). We may imagine through what forces the initiation into the creative might of the universe was carried out and what cultural impulses must have streamed forth from such a place as this. The plan of Newgrange, with the three chambers that have so far been excavated, is not unlike that in the Mexican picture shown here of the seven caves. Here, too, "guardians" stand at the entrance. In Newgrange in Ireland the guardian is the mighty threshold stone, engraved with spirals; in the Toltec picture there are several figures, among them presumably the one who is to be initiated. Between two of them speech goes to and fro, depicted in vortex trains and spirals. The same is repeated between the two figures within the cave; the motif also appears

The seven caves. From the Toltec legend of the original home of the race (after Seler)

in the entrance to the seven caves and in their edging. The way of approach to the mysteries of the seven caves is marked by foot-prints; access is obviously only possible by passing the sentinels and traversing the threshold of the flow of the forces of speech. Surely it is this stream of forces which is pictured on the stone at the threshold of the Newgrange tumulus.

Plate 82 depicts a remnant of Celtic culture in Central Europe, a stone engraved with many of the forms we now know so well. – In connection with this the above sketch shows a theme from early European times. The animal, with its characteristic movements, is developed out of the vortex.

The early Christians, too, initiated into the mystery of the Creation, knew of the real creative Word of the universe, which took on human form (Plate 87). What is depicted in detail in Plate 87 is expressed with more primitive means in the accompanying sketch simply as the movements of the word of the universe emanating from the sun. Plate 38 shows a capital from the Romanesque church in Oberstenfeld in Württemberg, on which we see the "spirits of the four corners of the earth" pouring forth bread and wine and the tree of life (fleur-de-lis motif) out of the stream of speech. According to Seitz the fleur-de-lis motif is the last remnant of the ancient representations of the Tree of Life. We restrict ourselves here to a few typical examples. Many more can be found among all peoples whose culture still has a real relation to the creative forces of the universe.

Animal ornaments from the Stone Age, developed from the vortex (after Schuchardt)

Cross-pillar at Reask (Ireland)

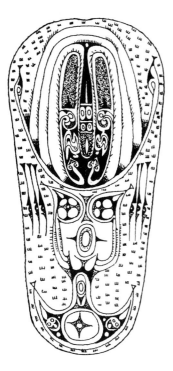

The art of the last few centuries shows how these secrets have withdrawn more and more from the consciousness of humanity. But may we not regard the return to the simplest elements of form and movement in modern art as an expression of the longing for the lost creative origin of man and the world? Do not many things in the agitated, disjointed quality of modern art show something of the battle to regain the picture of humanity created out of the archetypal elements of the word? May it not be that a new picture of man is struggling to be born out of the obscurity of the human soul? We think that the spiritual science developed by Rudolf Steiner can give the artist, too, answers to these questions.

By proceeding consistently in natural scientific thinking to the living reality, our modern consciousness may be widened and extended to compass the mysteries of the world. Proceeding along such a path we may attain a new conception of the nature of man which will open up new sources of inspiration, and not least for the artist. It is the path leading to a spiritual contemplation of the creative archetypal word, which brings forth man and nature out of the harmony of the universal alphabet.

Dance shield of painted wood (Trobriand Islands) British Museum, London

Design on a palm leaf (May River, New Guinea) Völkerkundliches Museum, Basel

136

INDEX OF ILLUSTRATIONS

21 An oyster shell with its countless layers of limestone seems to have been deposited out of the flowing movements of water itself. By the shape of these "deposits" an expert is able to tell the kind of movement present in the water in which it was formed.

22 Bell-shaped forms, which travel along with the current, arise in water flowing round a submerged stone. They are here made visible by stirring up fine clay in the water.

23 Train of vortices behind an obstacle in a muddy stream.

24 When water flows through an opening into still water the vortices form a rhythmical pattern.

25 Trains of vortices also arise if a solid object is drawn in a straight line through stationary liquid.

26 The vortices push into the surrounding liquid like the ball part of a joint into its socket. A suitable length of exposure reveals a delicate structure ("lines of force") which also passes across the dividing surfaces.

27 Train of vortices behind a thin rod.

28 Train of vortices behind a wide rod.

29 A rod drawn slowly and in a straight line through a viscous fluid causes a simple, wavy form.

30 The rod moves faster and the wave line becomes more pronounced.

31 Forms which arise if the rod is drawn through the water twice, the second time immediately after the first.

32 If the rod is drawn through the water several times at short intervals, complicated forms arise. Many small forms in a streaming connection with one another lie embedded in a large form.

33 A suitable length of exposure has revealed something of the structure of a train of vortices. A meandering stream winds its way between the separate vortices.

34 A structure similar to that of a train of vortices may often be seen in the bark and knots of a tree trunk. Trunk of a cypress tree.

35 Turbulent currents caused by a grating.

36 The grain in the trunk of an olive tree.

37 Water obstructed by a projection forms a rapidly revolving vortex. A vortex arising behind a board obstructing the current. The direction of the stream is from the top to the bottom of the picture.

38 Trunk of a mountain oak. Despite the hardness of the material the forms reveal their origin in the movements of the liquid element.

39 In the open sea mighty vortices can arise in which the whole dynamic force of the suction centre becomes visible.

40 The spiralling movement of vortices may be seen even in the hard rock of glacial pot-holes.

41 A photograph of a vortex taken under water reveals the spiralling surface between the water and the air which is being sucked in.

42–43   Even though they grow very slowly, snail shells still give an impressive picture of the dynamic force of the vortex.

44   The unfurling of fern leaves.

45   In many plants the rolled up form opens out into the flat area of the leaves. Shoot of a lily of the valley.

46–47   Two different stages of an *under*-water stream of liquid flowing into still water.

48   The slightest variations in the previous experiment create an abundance of new forms.

49–52   A stream of liquid flowing into still water. A series of pictures of the first stages.

53–54   Many shapes of organic formations here appear still purely in *movement*. Boundary surface formations between still and moving water.

55–58   A vortex ring rising upwards through water has a star-like form whose inner structure becomes visible when it "collides" with the surface.

59   A drop of water falling into a surface of still water causes a star-shaped figure to arise.

60   An ascending vortex ring shaped like a bell.

61   The effect on a flame sensitive to the sound of a note played on the organ. Increasing tone.

62–66   Experiments with air: streams of air or gas sensitive to sound issuing from small openings are moulded differently according to the source of the sound. Effect of the spoken vowels a, e, i, o, u.

67–70   Different musical instruments mould the sensitive flame differently and make the quality of the timbre visible (same pitch). 67 well bowed violin, 68 badly bowed violin, 69 flute, 70 French horn.

71   Warm air welling up over the land becomes visible in towering cloud formations.

72   Approaching storm.

73   Mackerel clouds beginning to form ripple formations (cf. Plate 8).

74   Endless variations of cloud forms.

75   Many forms found in water may also be found in the clouds.

76   Descending hail clouds.

77   "Rapids" in air currents. When wind blows across mountain ridges, wave formations appear at great heights.

78   Mackerel clouds in reverse: instead of flakes there appear hollows.

79   The same forms often arise whether air mingles with water or water with air.
Air snatched into water sparkles in droplets in the stream.

80   Water precipitated into the air makes sparkling drops in the play of the wind.

81   Threshold stone at the entrance to the Newgrange tumulus (Ireland).

82 Celtic pillar at Pfalzfeld.

83 Stone of Gotland (Sweden).

84–85 Greek grave stelae.

86 Christ's family tree. Detail of the bronze doors of San Zeno, Verona.

87 Crucifixion. Bronze relief, Ireland, 8th-century.

88 Romanesque capital in the church of Oberstenfeld (Württemberg). The "spirits of the four corners of the earth" cause bread and wine and the tree of life to flow forth in their stream of speech.

ACKNOWLEDGMENTS

The following photographs and illustrations were kindly provided by:—
Akademische Druck- und Verlagsanstalt, Graz: Toltec picture of the seven caves. Archeological Museum, Athens: Plate 85. Historical Museum, Stockholm: Plate 83. KLM Aerocarto, Amsterdam: Plate 10 (aerial photograph). National Museum of Ireland, Dublin: Plate 87. K. Paysan, Stuttgart: Plate 15. Ray Delvert, Villeneuve-sur-Lot: Plate 1 (aerial photograph). Rheinisches Landesmuseum, Bonn: Plate 82. W. Roggenkamp, Stuttgart: Plates 7, 8, 11, 12, 13, 16, 17, 38, 44, 45, 84. P. E. Schiller, Dornach (Switzerland): Plates 61 to 70. K. Stülcken, Hamburg-Rissen: Plate 14. Ullstein Bilderdienst, Berlin: Plate 39.
Plates by the author: 2 to 6, 9, 18 to 37, 40 to 43, 46 to 60, 71 to 81, 86, 88.

Photographic method used for Plates 25 to 32:

For the purpose of illustrating the formation of trains of vortices in water as clearly as possible, the speed of the process can be slackened by the addition of a viscous fluid (e.g. glycerine). A rod, held vertical, is drawn in a straight line through the still water in a shallow basin. It is easier to observe or photograph the process if the surface of the water is dusted with a fine powder (e.g. lycopodium). Depending on the measurements of the rod and the speed at which it is moved, the resulting train of vortices in the water is more or less marked.

BIBLIOGRAPHY

Abel, O.: Lehrbuch der Paläozoologie. Jena 1924.

Adams, G., and Whicher, O.: The Plant between Sun and Earth. Goethean Science Foundation 1952. Die Pflanze in Raum und Gegenraum. Stuttgart 1960.

Autrum, H.: Schallempfang bei Tier und Mensch. Die Naturwissenschaften 1942, 5/6.

Aymar, G. C.: Herrlicher Vogelflug. Thun 1949.

Baschin, O.: Gleitflächengesetz und Flußmäander. Die Naturwissenschaften 1926, 18.

Bautzmann, H., and Schroeder, R.: Die Motorik des Amnions. Umschau 1954, 3.

Békésy, G.: Über die Schwingungen der Schneckentrennwand beim Präparat und Ohrmodell. Akustische Zeitschrift 1942, 6.

Békésy, G.: Zur Theorie des Hörens. Physikalische Zeitschrift 1928, 22.

Benninghoff, A.: Spaltlinien am Knochen, eine Methode zur Ermittlung der Architektur platter Knochen. Anatomischer Anzeiger 1925, p. 189.

Berg, B.: Mit den Zugvögeln nach Afrika. Berlin 1933.

Böker, H.: Einführung in die vergleichende biologische Anatomie der Wirbeltiere. Jena 1935, 1937.

Bortels, H.: Beziehungen zwischen Witterungsablauf, physikalisch-chemischen Reaktionen, biologischem Geschehen und Sonnenaktivität. Die Naturwissenschaften 1951, 8.

Braem, M.: Odyssee der wandernden Tiere. Stuttgarter Zeitung, 5th October, 1957.

Buch, K.: Kohlensäure in Atmosphäre und Meer. Annalen der Hydrographie und maritimen Meteorologie, 1942, VII.

Buddenbrock, W. v.: Grundriß der vergleichenden Physiologie. Berlin 1939.

Bülow, K. v.: Erdgeschichte am Wege. Stuttgart 1941.

Carrière, Z.: Flammes chantantes. Revue d'Acoustique 1936, 3/4.

Carson, R. L.: The Sea around us. London 1951.

Chromow, S. P.: Einführung in die synoptische Wetteranalyse. Vienna 1942.

Clara, M.: Entwicklungsgeschichte des Menschen. Leipzig 1943.

Cloos, W.: Lebensstufen der Erde. Freiburg i.B., 1958.

Cocannouer, J. A.: Water and the Cycle of Life. New York 1958.

Colman, J. S.: The Sea and its Mysteries. London 1950.

Cook, T. A.: The Curves of Life. London 1914.

Defant, A., and others: Ebb and Flow: the tides of earth, air and water. Univ. of Michigan Press 1958.

Demoll, R.: Grundwasser, eine Lebensfrage. Umschau 1952, 1.

Demoll, R.: Ketten für Prometheus, gegen die Natur oder mit ihr? Munich 1954.

Dietrich, G.: Die Schwingungssysteme der halb- und eintägigen Tiden in den Ozeanen. Berlin 1944.

Dingler, H.: Die Bewegung der pflanzlichen Flugorgane. Munich 1889.

Eck, B.: Technische Strömungslehre. Berlin 1941.

Ehrhardt, A.: Das Watt. Hamburg 1937.

Eidmann, H.: Lehrbuch der Entomologie. Berlin 1941.

Fletcher, H.: Speech and Hearing in Communication. New York 1953.

Focke, H., Leege, O., and Schack, W.: Wunder des Möwenfluges. Frankfurt a. M. 1943.

Frisch, K. v.: Physiologie des Geruchs- und Geschmackssinnes. Berlin 1926.

Goerttler, K.: Die Entwicklung des menschlichen Kehlkopfes. Umschau 1955, 4.

Goethes naturwissenschaftliche Schriften, herausgegeben von R. Steiner. Stuttgart 1883.

Hansen, W.: Neuere Untersuchungen über Meeresströmungen. Die Naturwissenschaften 1954, 9.

Henderson, L. J.: Die Umwelt des Lebens. Wiesbaden 1914.

Henry, F.: Early Christian Irish Art. Dublin 1954.

Hesse, R., and Doflein, F.: Tierbau und Tierleben. Leipzig and Berlin 1910.

Hope, R. C.: Holy Wells of England. London 1893.

Horstmann, E.: Überindividuelle Lebensformen bei Staren und Kranichen. Umschau 1951, 16.

Huber, B.: Die Saftströme der Pflanzen. Berlin 1956.

Idrac, P.: Experimentelle Untersuchungen über den Segelflug. Munich and Berlin 1932.

Isaachsen, J.: Innere Vorgänge in Flüssigkeiten und Gasen. Zeitschrift VDI 1911.

Jacobs, W.: Fliegen, Schwimmen, Schweben. Berlin 1954.

Jenny, H.: Schwingungen experimentell sichtbar gemacht. Du (Switzerland) 1962, 9.

Kalle, K.: Der Stoffhaushalt des Meeres. Leipzig 1943.

Kaufmann, H.: Rhythmische Phänomenen der Erdoberfläche. Brunswick 1929.

Keidel, W. D.: Die Funktionsweise des menschlichen Gehörs. Umschau 1960, 3.

Kleinschmidt, E.: Über Aufbau und Entstehung von Zyklonen. Meteorologische Rundschau 1950, 1/2 and 1951, 5/6.

Koegel, L.: Stromriesen. Stuttgart 1947.

Kolisko, L.: Workings of the Stars in Earthly Substances. London 1928.

Kruse, W.: Wasser. Hanover 1949.

Krutzsch, C. H.: Über eine experimentell beobachtete Erscheinung an Wirbelringen. Dissertation, Dresden 1939.

Lehrs, E.: Man or Matter. London 1958.

Litzelmann, E.: Rheinkorrektion und Rheinseitenkanal. Umschau 1957, 5.

Locher-Ernst, L.: Raum und Gegenraum. Dornach, Switzerland 1957.

Löbsack, T.: Der Atem der Erde. Munich 1957.

Luchsinger, R. and Reich, W.: Stimmphysiologie und Stimmbildung. Vienna 1951.

Ludwig, W.: Rechts-Links-Problem. Berlin 1932.

Lüneburg, H.: Die Außensände. Umschau 1958, 23.

Markus, E.: Die Verteilung des Luftdrucks über der Erdoberfläche. Annalen der Hydrographie und Maritimen Meteorologie 1944, VI.

Mügge, R.: Registrierung von Erdbeben und Gezeiten durch unterirdisches Wasser. Umschau 1955, 11.

Müller, W.: Der "Pulsschlag" der Mineralquellen. Umschau 1951, 3.

Ninck, M.: Die Bedeutung des Wassers im Kult und Leben der Alten. Darmstadt 1960.

Novalis: Fragmente. Jena 1907.

Parlenko, G. E.: Oberflächenwellen auf einer in einem bewegten Tank enthaltenen Flüssigkeit. Phil. Mag. 1933., p. 360.

Pfeiffer, E.: Gesunde und kranke Landschaft. Berlin 1942.

Poppelbaum, H.: Der Bildekräfteleib der Lebewesen als Gegenstand wissenschaftlicher Erfahrung. Stuttgart 1924.

Poppelbaum, H.: Man and Animal. London 1931.

Poppelbaum, H.: Tier-Wesenskunde. Dornach 1954.

Prandtl, L.: Essentials of Fluid Dynamics. London 1952.

Prandtl, L., and Tietjens, O.: Applied hydro- and aeromechanics. London 1934.

Raethjen, P.: Dynamik der Zyklonen. Leipzig 1953.

Rinne, F.: Über Wellengleitung im Großen und im Kleinen. Leipzig 1925.

Roll, H. U: Wellen und Wellenwirkungen an der Küste. Umschau 1953, 14.

Rutter, F.: Grundriß der Limnologie. Berlin 1962.

Schieferstein, H.: Resonanzflug. Zeitschrift für Flugtechnik und Motorluftschiffahrt 1925, 5.

Schiller, P. E.: Untersuchungen an der freien schallempfindlichen Flamme. Akustische Zeitschrift 1938, 1.

Schmauß, A.: Kalendermäßige Bindungen im Wettergeschehen. Forschungen und Fortschritte 1936, 12 and 1939, 12.

Schmauß, A.: Wiederkehrende Wetterwendepunkte. Forschungen und Fortschritte 1940, 15.

Schmauß, A.: Biologische Gedanken in der Meteorologie. Forschungen und Fortschritte 1945, 1–6.

Schmeil, O.: Textbook of Zoology, various editions.

Schmidt, C. W.; Der Fluß, eine Morphologie fließender Gewässer. Leipzig, no date.

Schmidt, R.: Flug und Flieger im Pflanzen- und Tierreich. Berlin. 1939.

Schmitt, C.: Der Teich und sein Leben. Stuttgart 1948.

Schuchardt, C.: Alteuropa. Berlin 1944.

Schüpbach, W.: Pflanzengeometrie. Bern 1944.

Schwenk, T.: Grundlagen der Potenzforschung. Schwäbisch Gmünd 1954.

Schwenk, T.: Über rhythmische Vorgänge in der Natur. Weleda-Nachrichten 1954, 34.

Schwenk, T.: Von der Hygiene im Lebensgeschehen der Erde. Weleda-Nachrichten 1956, 42.

Schwenk, T.: Von der Rhythmik in den Gewässern und im Menschenohr. Die Drei 1961, 1.

Seitz, F.: Die Irminsul. Pähl (Upper Bavaria) 1953.

Steiner, R.: Theosophy. London 1954.

Steiner, R.: An Outline of Occult Science. London 1963.

Steiner, R.: Von Seelenrätseln. Dornach 1960.

Steiner, R.: Man as Symphony of the Creative Word. 12 lectures, London 1945.

Steiner, R.: Eurythmie als Impuls für künstlerisches Betätigen und Betrachten. Dornach 1953.

Steiner, R.: Eurythmy as Visible Speech. London 1956.

Teichmann, H.: Wettereinfluß von Atomexplosionen als Störung periodischer Strömungen in der Stratosphäre. Die Naturwissenschaften. 1954, 21.

Thienemann, A.: Die Binnengewässer in Natur und Kultur. Berlin 1955.

Thorade, H.: Ebbe und Flut. Berlin 1941.

Tyndall, J.: Sound. 8 lectures delivered at the Royal Inst. of Great Britain. 1867.

Tyndall, J.: The Forms of Water in Clouds and Rivers, Ice and Glaciers. 1872.

Veltheim-Ostrau, H. v.: Tagebücher aus Asien. Cologne 1951.

Vergleichende Anatomie der Wirbeltiere von Ihle u. a. Berlin 1927.

Vernadsky, W. J.: Geochemie. Leipzig 1930.

Vogt, H. H.: Die Plitvitzer Seen. Kosmos 1960, 8.

Wachsmuth, G.: Etheric Formative Forces in Cosmos, Earth and Man. London 1932.

Wachsmuth, G.: Erde und Mensch. Kreuzlingen 1952.

Wachsmuth, G.: Die Entwicklung der Erde. Dornach 1950.

Wagner, G.: Einführung in die Erden- und Landschaftsgeschichte. Öhringen 1960.

Walden, H.: Welche Eigenschaften besitzt eine neu aufkommende Dünung? Umschau 1955, 20.

Walter, F.: Experimentelle und theoretische Untersuchungen über die Strömungsformen hinter scharfkantigen Widerstandskörpern . . . Leipzig 1940.

Weiland, H.: Der Malpane-Fluß. Zeitschrift VDI 1938, 51.

Weimann, R.: Verschmutzte Wasserläufe. Stuttgart 1958.

Weissenberg, R., and Michaelis, L.: Entwicklungsgeschichte des Menschen. Leipzig 1929.

Weyher, C. L.: Sur les tourbillons. Paris 1889.

Wissman, H. v.: Über seitliche Erosion. Bonn 1951.

Wittmann, H.: Wasser- und Geschiebebewegung in gekrümmten Flußstrecken. Berlin 1938.

Wöhlisch, E.: Das Wesen der kautschukartigen Hochelastizität. Umschau 1950, 3.

Wundt, W.: Gewässerkunde. Berlin, Göttingen, Heidelberg 1953.

Zietschmann, O.: Der Darmkanal der Säugetiere. Anatomischer Anzeiger 1925, p. 155.

1

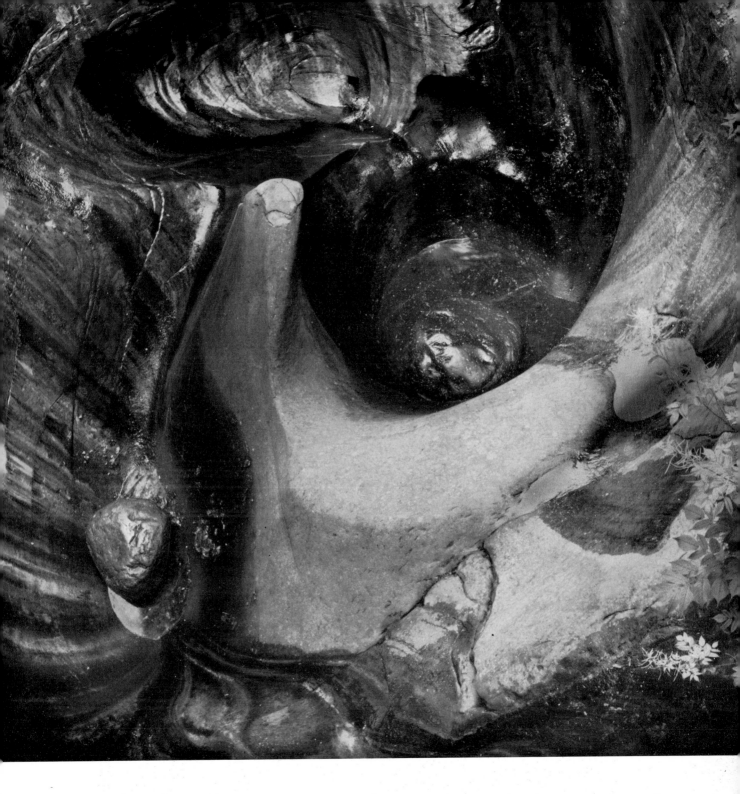

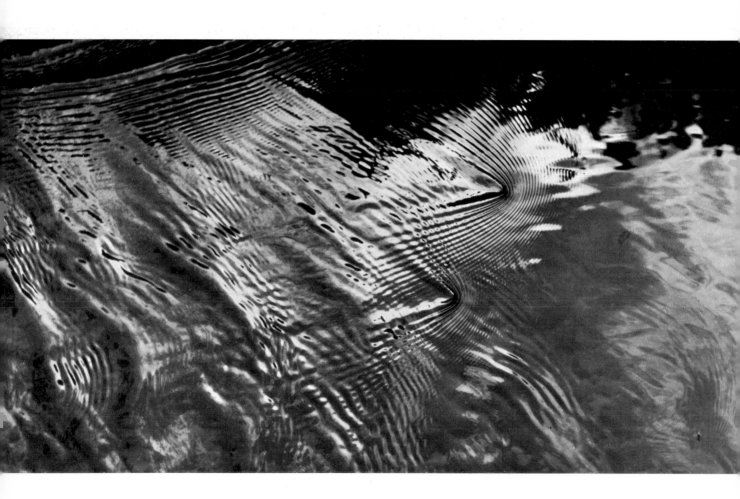

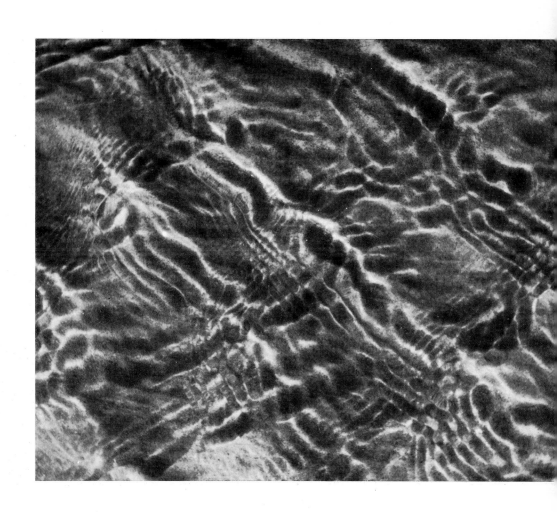

8

9

10
11

12

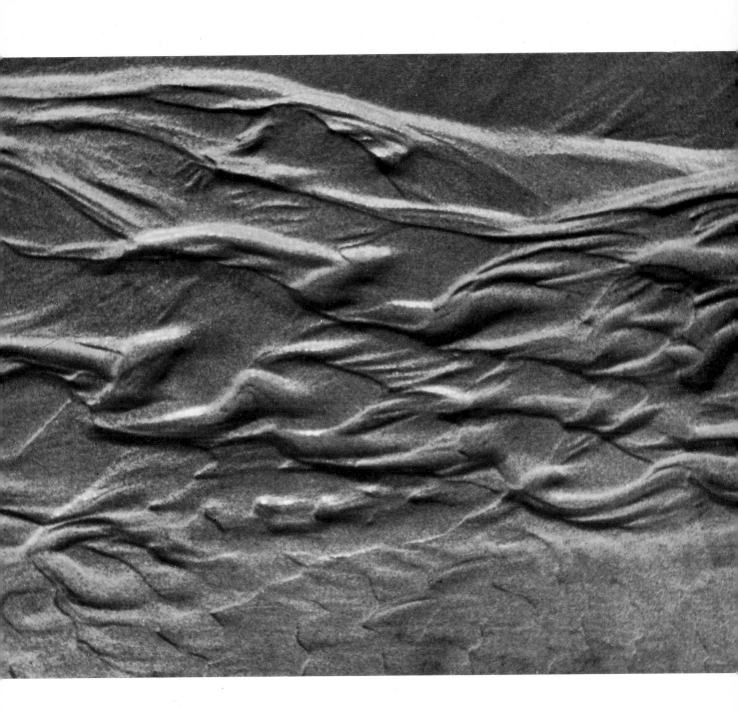

13

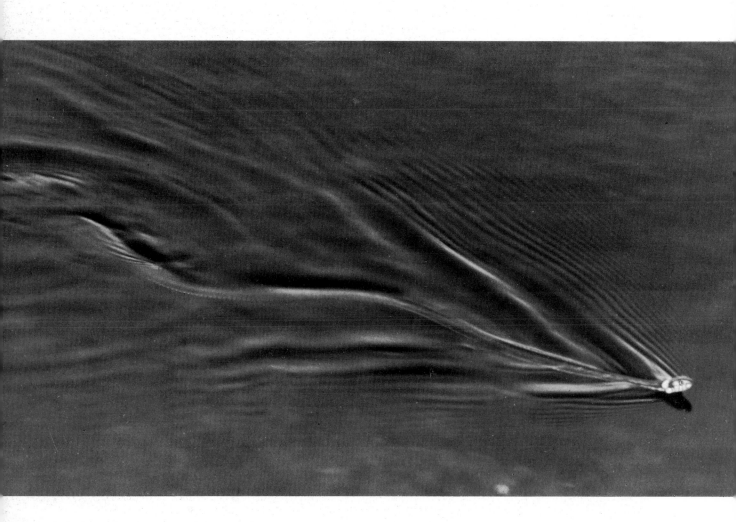

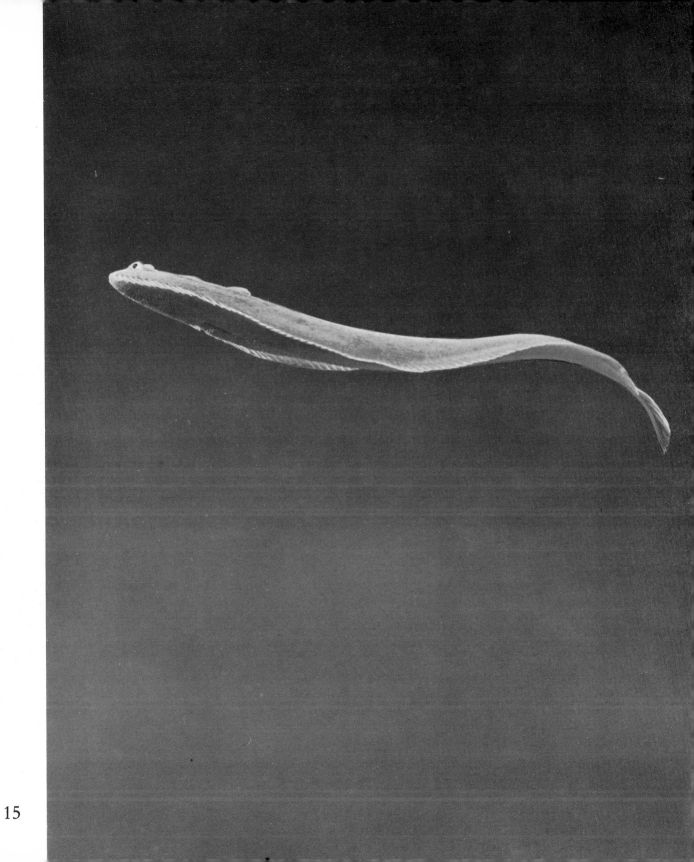

15

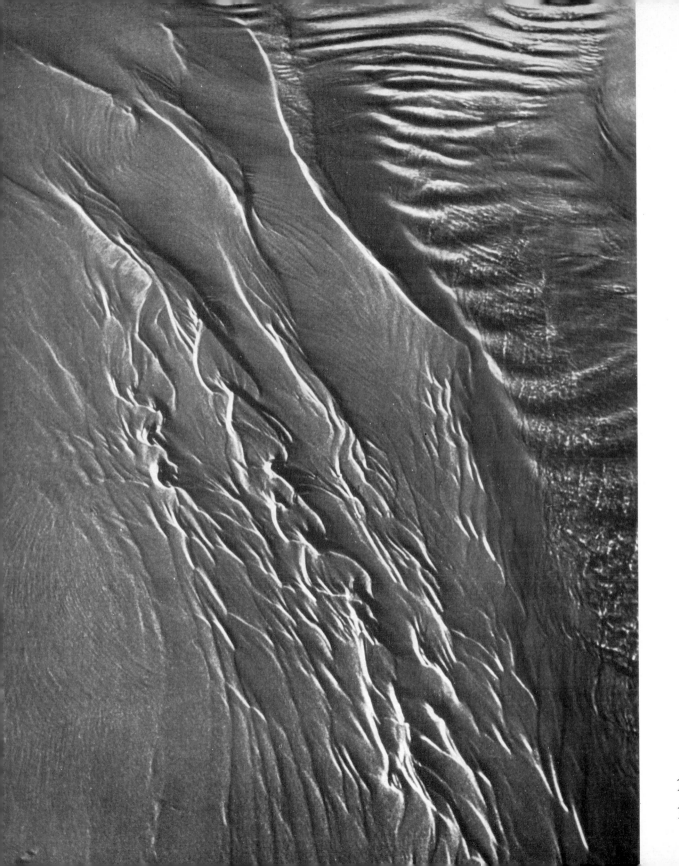

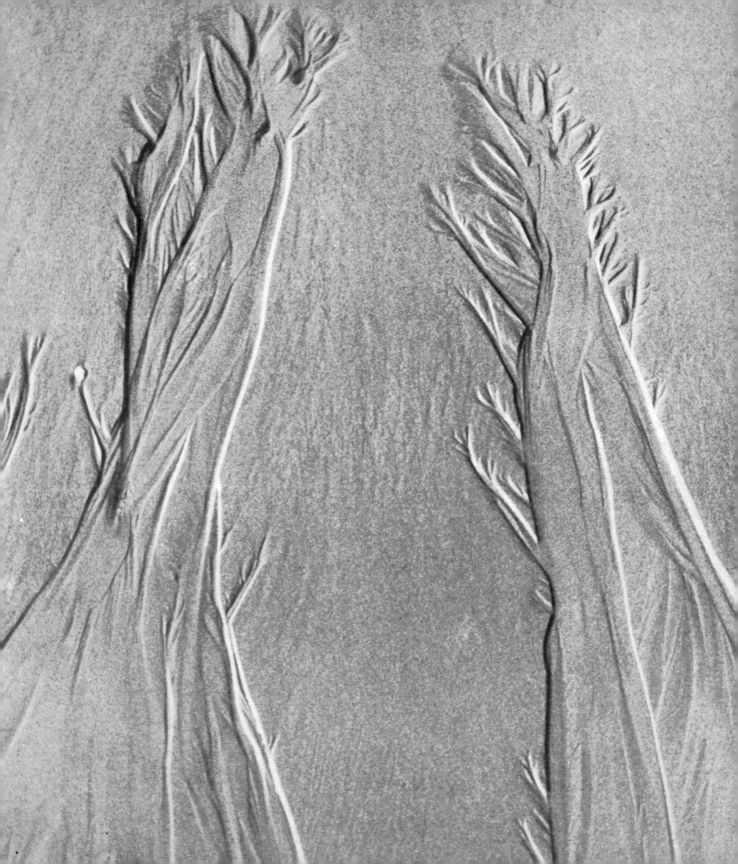

18

19

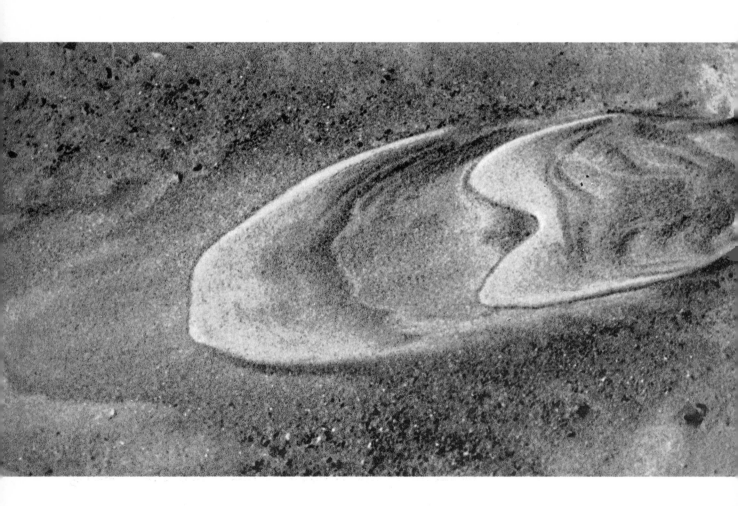

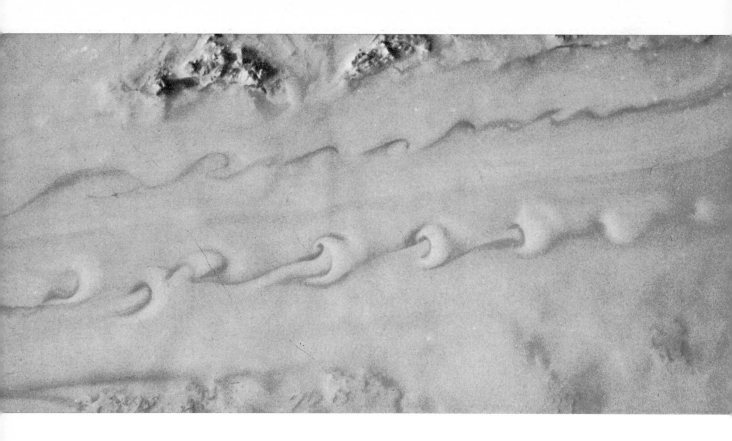

22

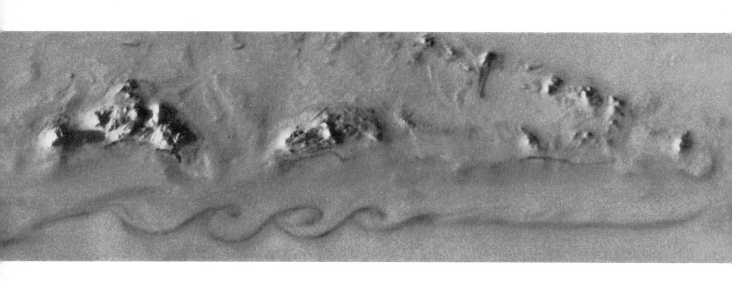

23

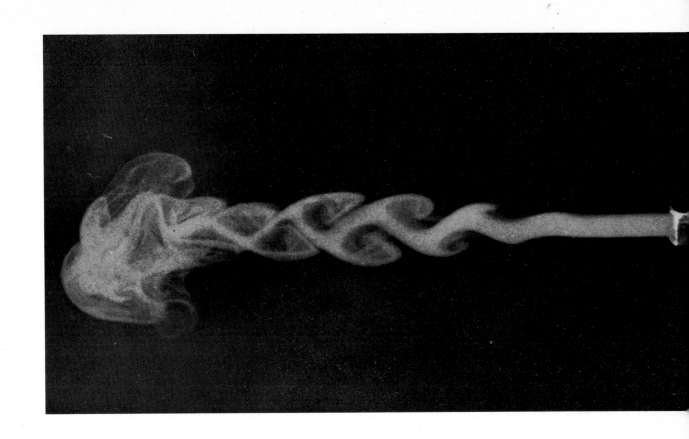

25

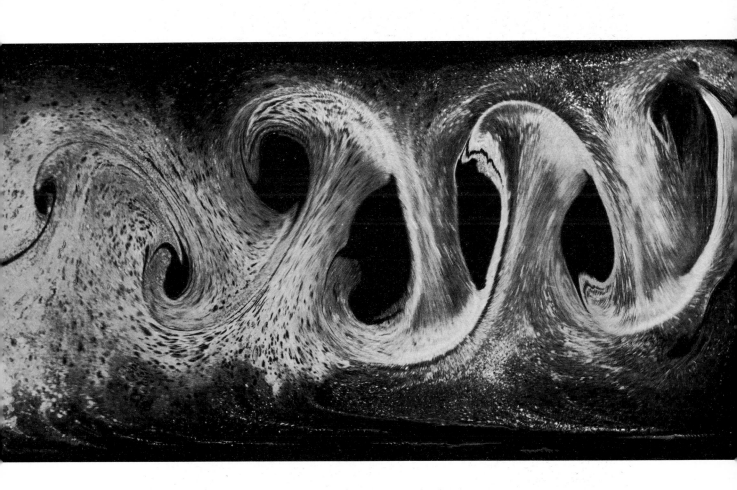

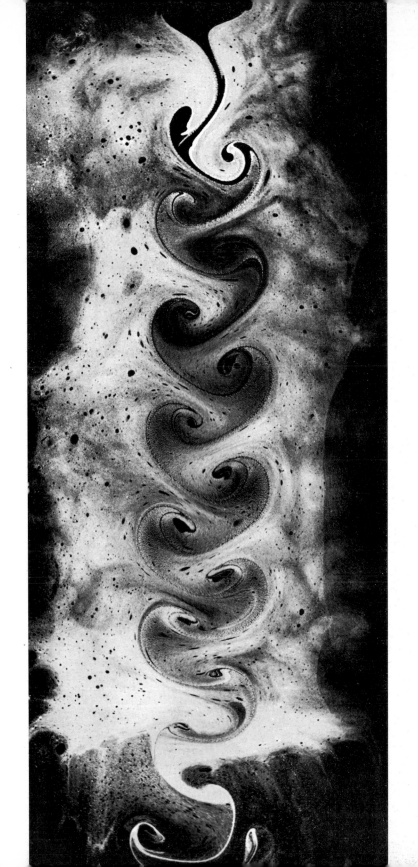

27

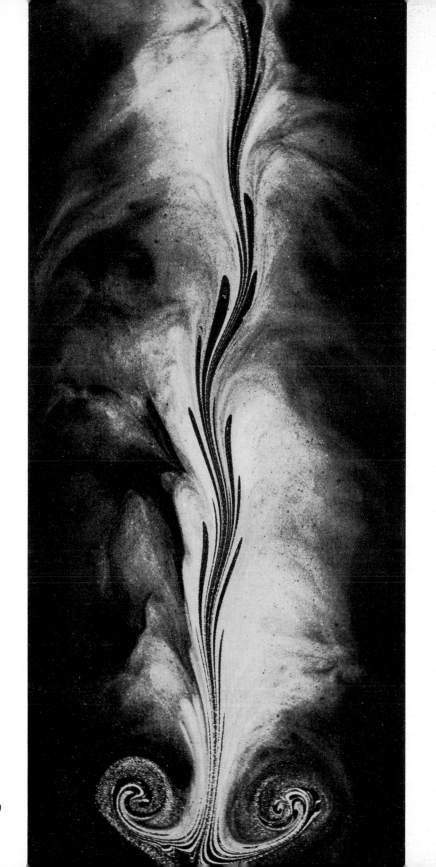

29

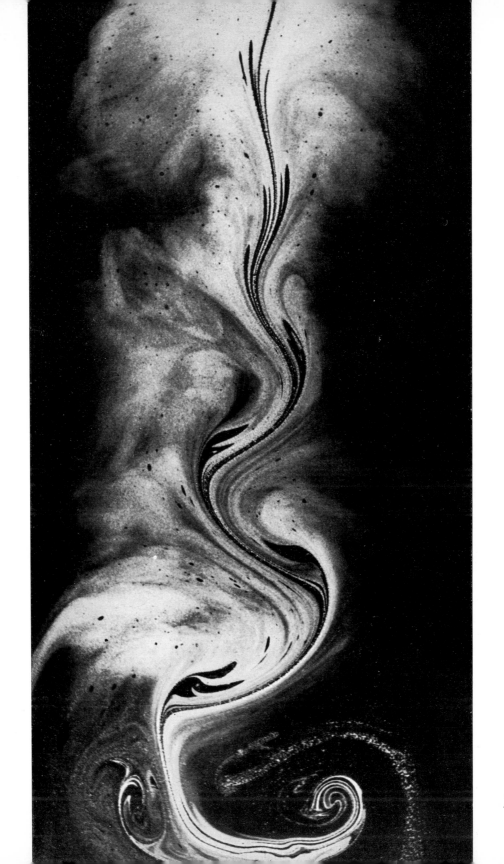

30

31

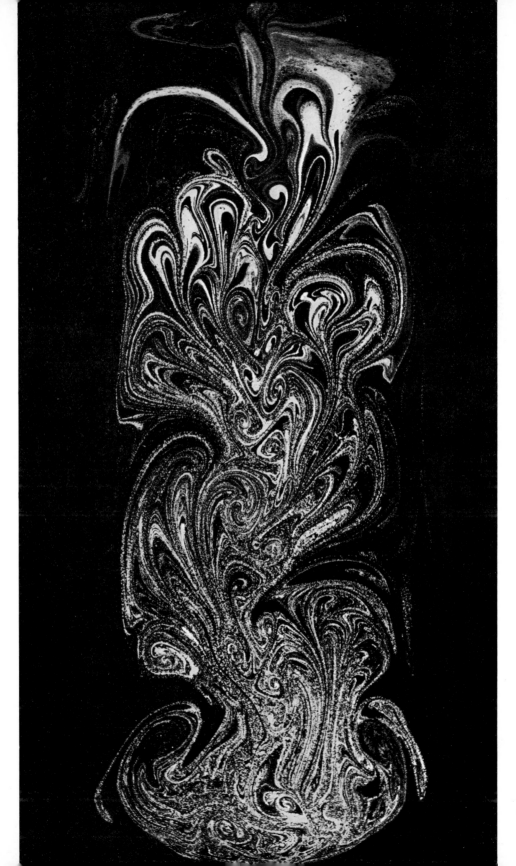

32

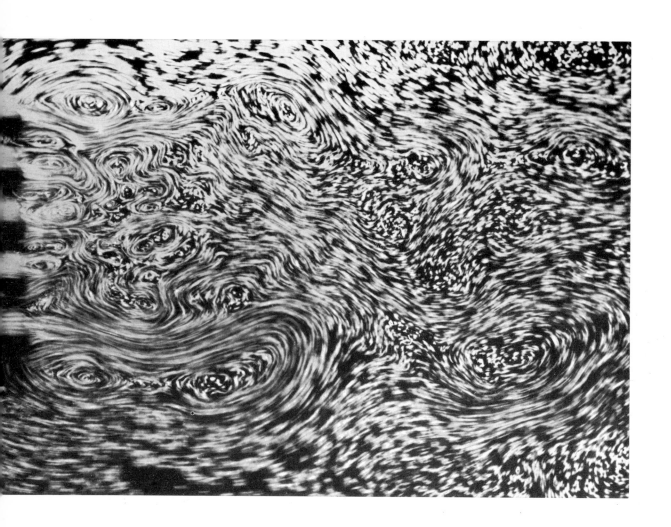

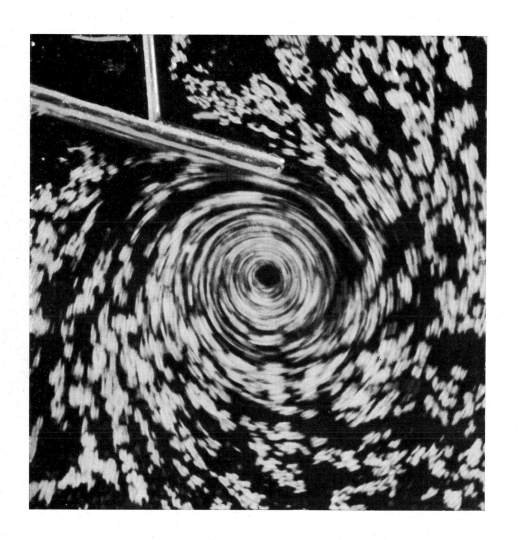

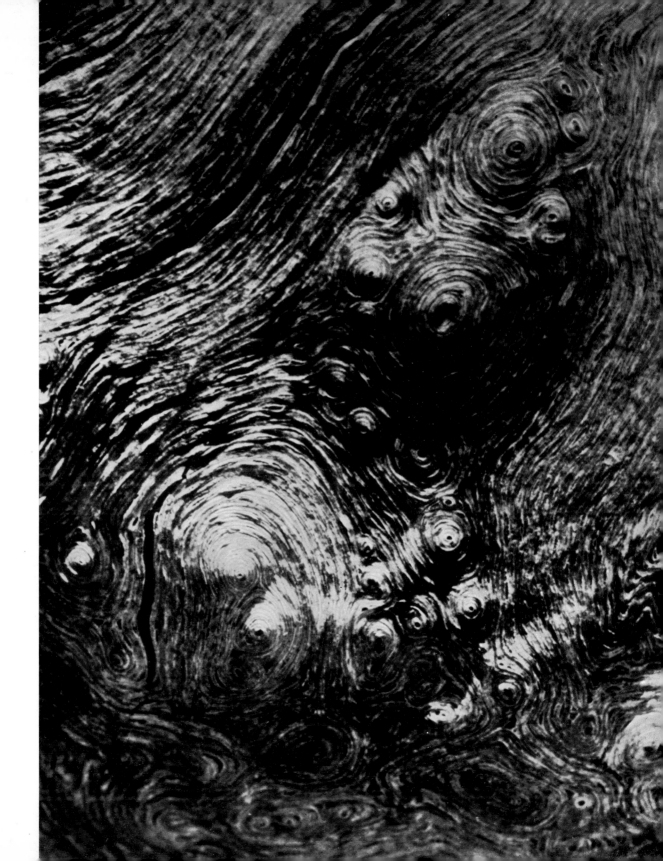

38

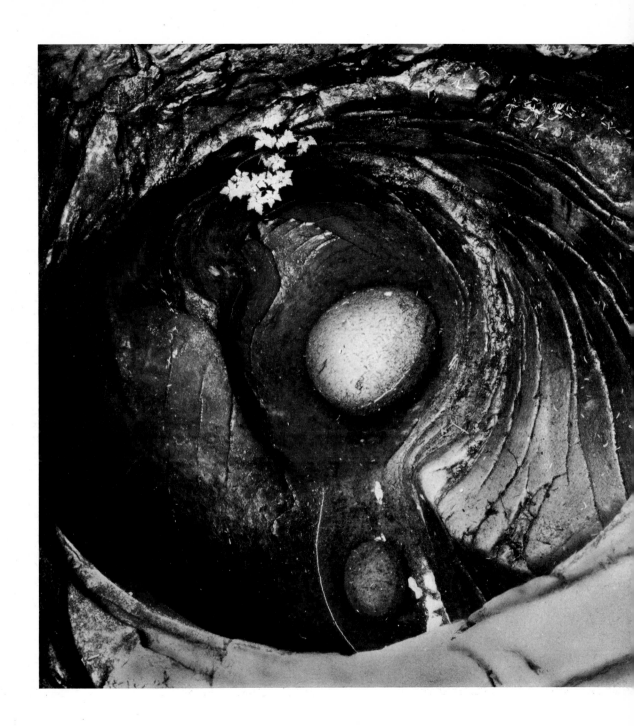

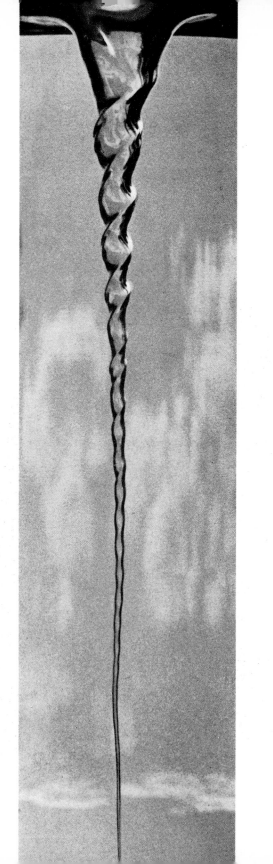
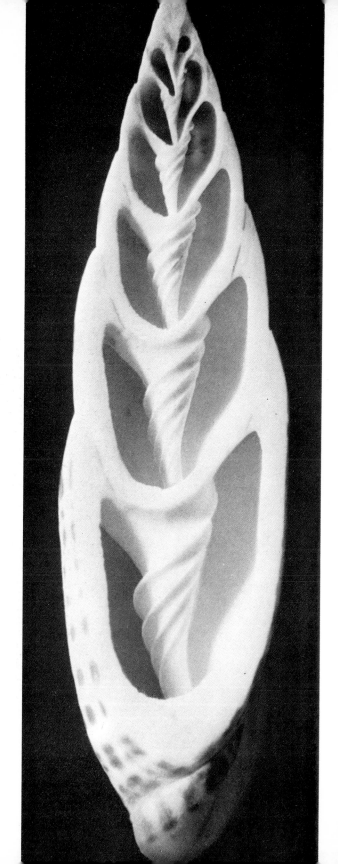

41

42

43

44

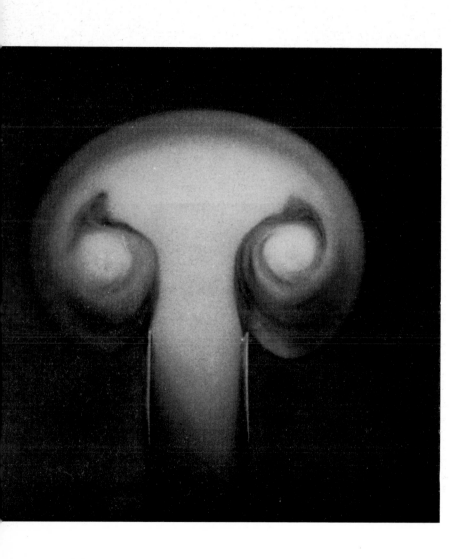

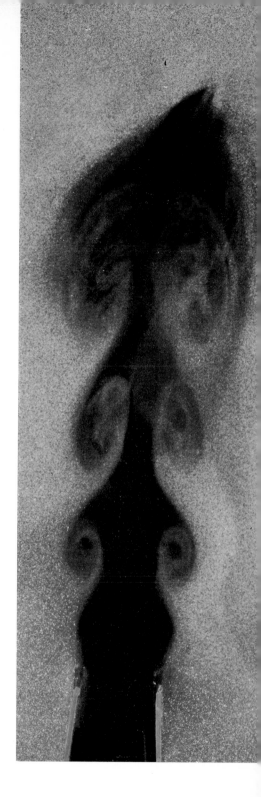

46

47

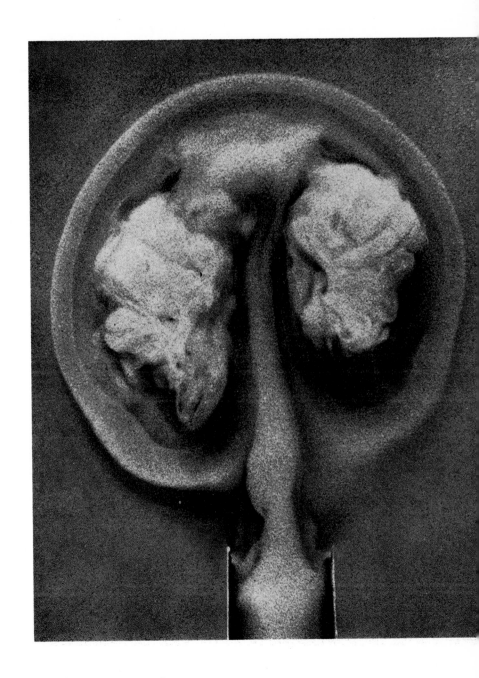

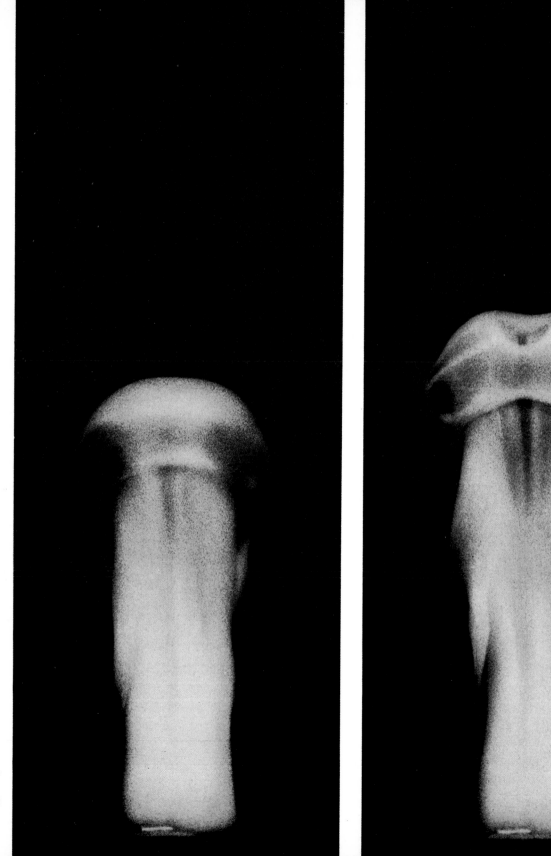

49
50

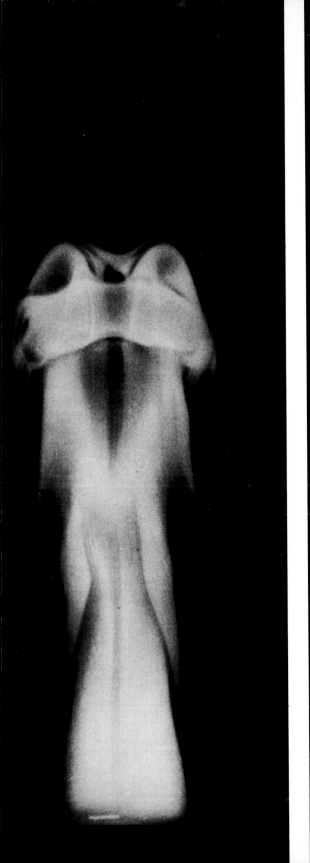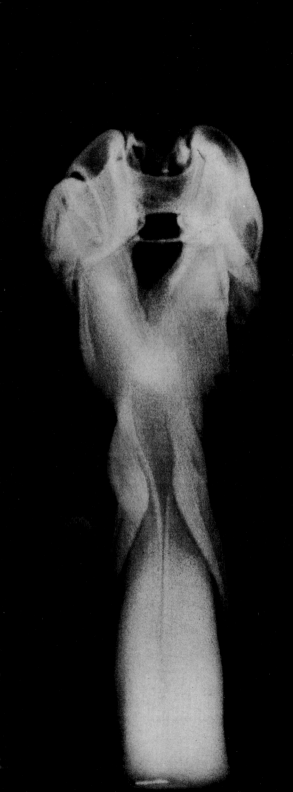

51
52

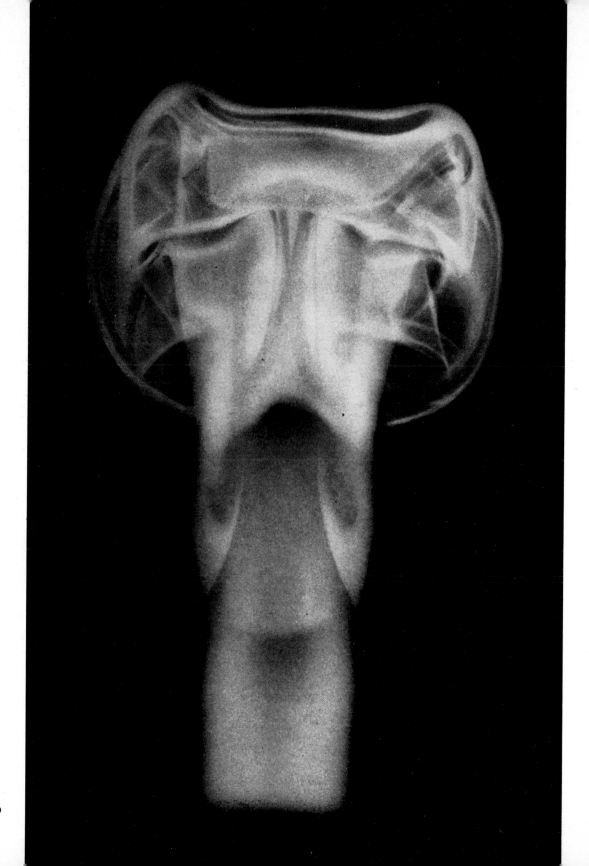

53

54

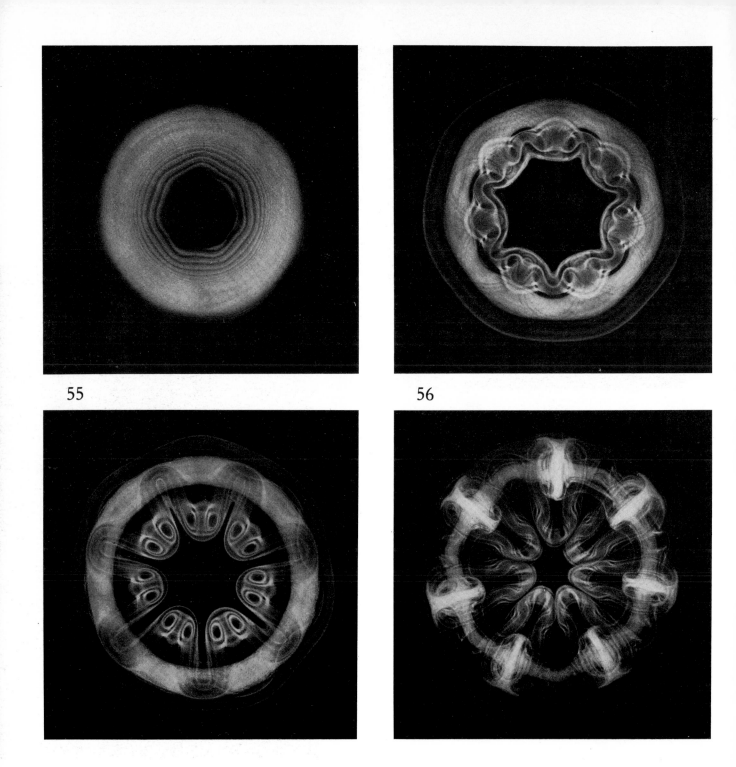

55

56

57

58

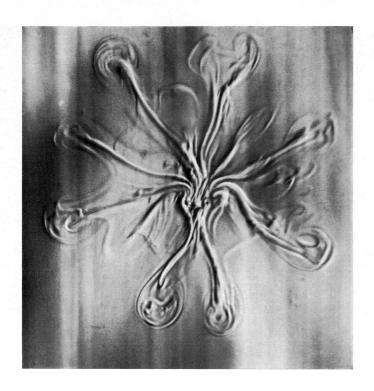

59

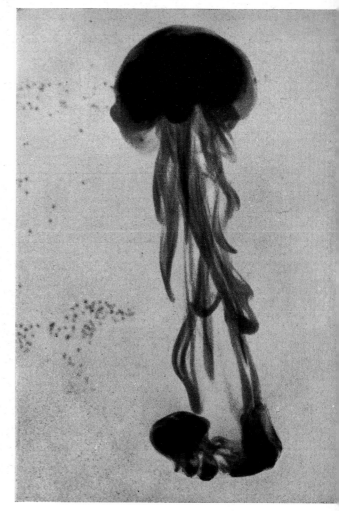

60

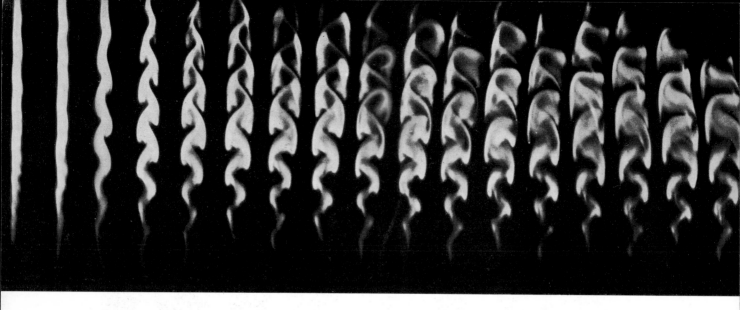

61 Organ note increasing in volume

62 A   63 E   64 I   65 O   66 U

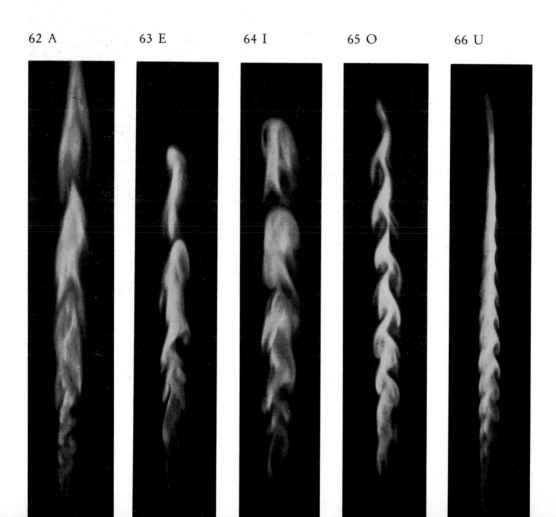

| 67 | 68 | 69 | 70 |

Well bowed
Violin

Badley bowed
Violin

Flute

French horn

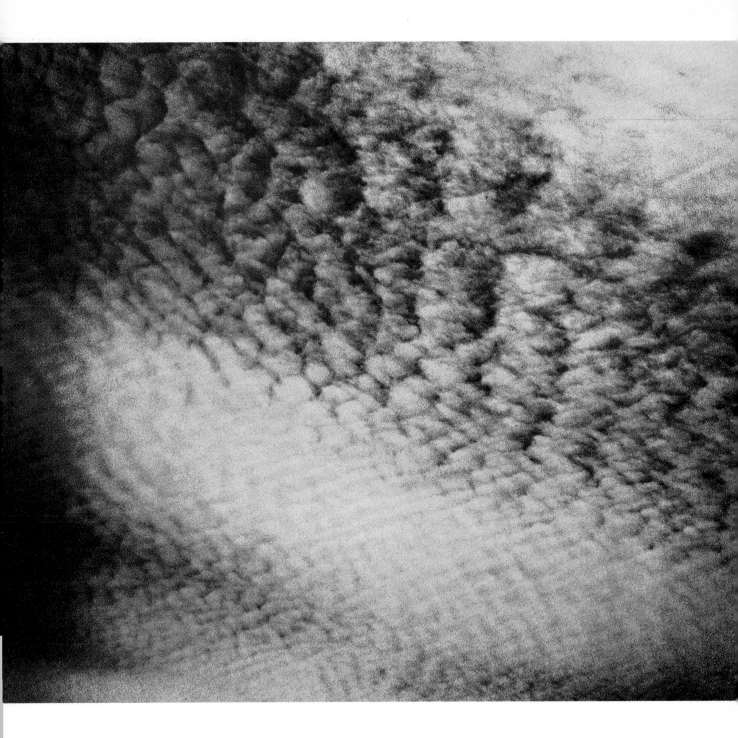

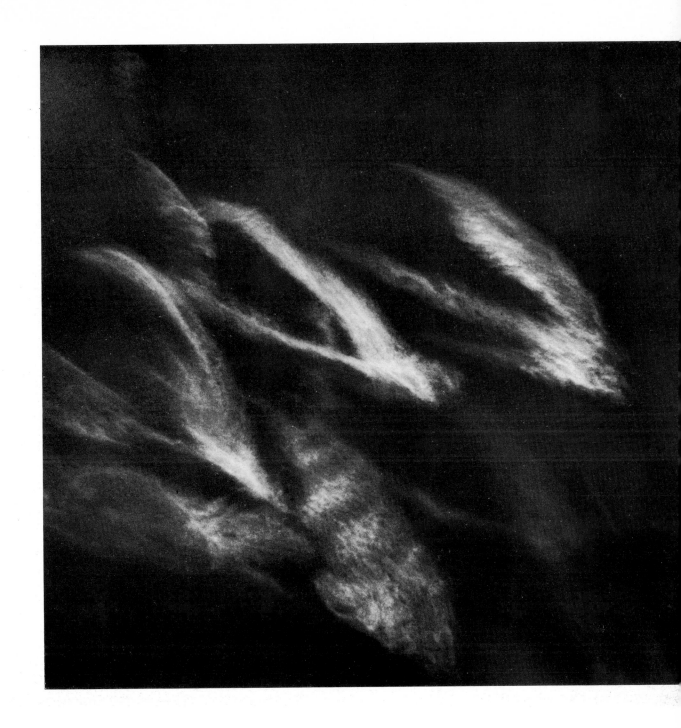

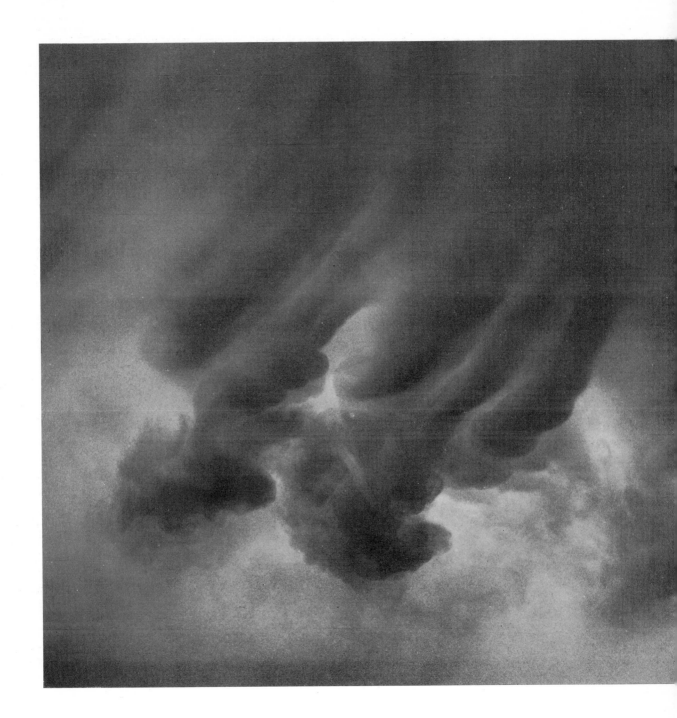

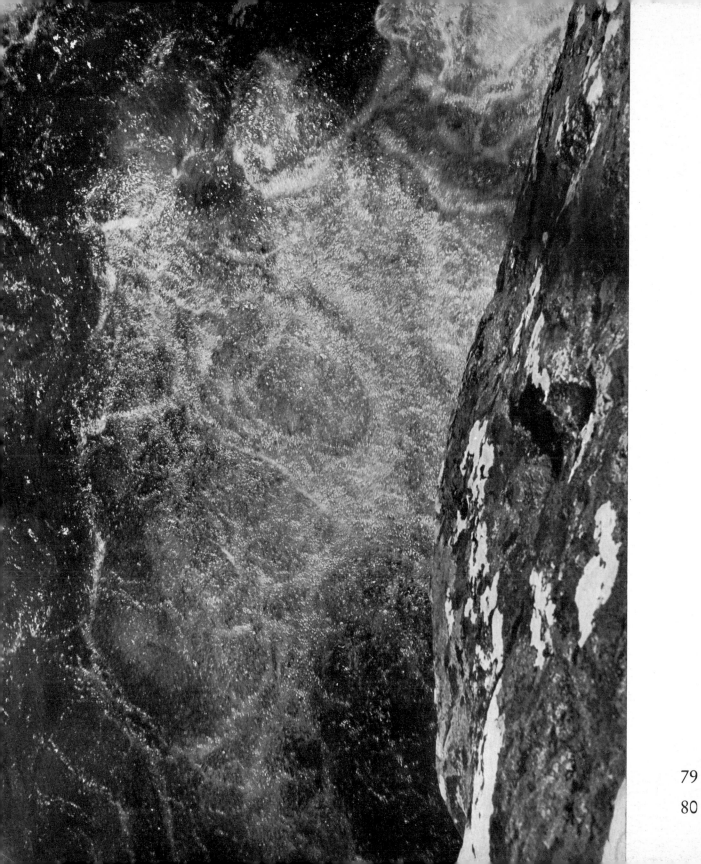

79

80

Wem die Natur
ihr offenbares Geheimnis
zu enthüllen anfängt,
der empfindet eine unwiderstehliche
Sehnsucht nach ihrer würdigsten
Auslegerin, der Kunst.

He to whom Nature
begins to reveal
her open secret
will feel an irresistible yearning
for her most worthy interpreter,
Art.

                    Goethe

82

83

85